W9-DBW-752

Rethinking Leadership:
A Collection of Articles

by
Thomas J. Sergiovanni

with a Foreword by
Theodore R. Sizer

WITHDRAWN

SkyLight
Training and Publishing Inc.

CARL A. RUDISILL LIBRARY
LENOIR-RHYNE COLLEGE

HD
57.7
.S457
1999
May 1999

Rethinking Leadership: A Collection of Articles

Published by SkyLight Training and Publishing Inc.
2626 S. Clearbrook Dr., Arlington Heights, IL 60005-5310
Phone 800-348-4474, 847-290-6600
Fax 847-290-6609
info@iriskylight.com
http://www.iriskylight.com

Senior Vice President, Product Development: Robin Fogarty
Director, Product Development: Ela Aktay
Acquisitions Editor: Jean Ward
Editor: Sue Schumer
Cover Designer and Illustrator: David Stockman
Book Designer: Donna Ramirez
Indexer: McVey & Associates
Production Supervisor: Bob Crump
Production Assistant: Christina Georgi

© 1999 SkyLight Training and Publishing Inc.
All rights reserved.
Printed in the United States of America.

ISBN 1-57517-148-1
LCCCN 98-61713

2355-McN
Item number 1707

ZYXWVUTSRQPONMLKJIHGFEDCBA
06 05 04 03 02 01 00 99   15 14 13 12 11 10 9 8 7 6 5 4 3 2 1

ontents

Foreword

ND WHAT KIND OF LEADERS SHALL THERE BE?
Americans have a love affair with *leadership*. Who could be
against that? We admire the take-charge individual. All our
graduate students will be leaders. Programs in Educational Administration have been renamed Programs in Educational Leadership. We
often hear the petition: American education needs leadership. We
hear America needs leadership. He is a leader; let's elect him. She is a
leader; we need her to take charge. We train *leaders,* not followers.

Each of us is for leadership as long as those who embody it face
in what we believe to be a proper direction. Strong folks who march
to different drummers are dangerous. A leader, then, is one who
espouses what we believe needs to be done. If he is in charge, then I
can get aboard. Jesse Helms and not Ted Kennedy, Ted Kennedy and
not Jesse Helms. The Christian Coalition and not the National Organization for Women, NOW and not the CC.

Most leaders are meant to be decisive. What have they done during their first one hundred days? If there is the appearance of movement, hurrahs for them. Leaders get results, measurable, visible
results—the easier to tote up the better. No quickly discernible
results? No leader.

Leaders are expected to be tough. They cut through old slovenly
ways. They rally us to the needed work. They discharge the rascals
and the pettifoggers. They are captains of getting things done, now.
They are all things to all people, listeners but eloquent, receptive but
persuasive, flexible but devoted to staying a course, principled but
decisive in uprooting the wicked. They are fighters but above the
fray. They are "up to date." They call leaders by their first names.

Is all this a caricature? Less than we care to admit. Our times tend to reward a George S. Patton-type leader more than a Mother Teresa-type leader. The nonphotogenic in this image-focused age have trouble persuading us that they can lead. The person who asks for time to think is dismissed as evasive.

Within public education no one has pondered these matters more systematically than has Tom Sergiovanni. He eschews the "take charge" imagery. He talks about leaders who make connections, who draw the best out of those around her or him. He makes the painful distinctions between leadership that cuts quickly to a particular, personally critical goal and leadership that emerges from the moral motives that transcend immediate targets. Surely Nelson Mandela is a hero for Sergiovanni: patient, principled, a man who acted and acts in the collective best interest even when short-term militance on his part might be applauded and tactically correct.

If one is of the tough guy school of leadership, Sergiovanni is not for you. He wants us to think, to ponder what is right for the long run and what is the common good. Trying to find or create that common good will itself be a controversial process. For Sergiovanni, effective leaders take time to listen, to sense, to gather, to articulate, to discern, to think, and thus to lead. May his followers multiply. May these essays help that multitude into being.

Theodore R. Sizer
Acting Principal, Francis W. Parker Charter
Essential School, Massachusetts, and
Chair of the Coalition of Essential Schools
October 1998

Prologue

On Rethinking Leadership: A Conversation With Tom Sergiovanni

by Ron Brandt

You write about *"substitutes for leadership." Are you really saying that leadership is an outdated concept?*
Not leadership; what's outdated is our understanding of it. We think of leadership as direct and interpersonal, and assume that we must have it. But there are many situations in which leadership is not an issue. I think that if we study those settings, we'll find that certain qualities can substitute for leadership.

Such as?
Norms. Commitments. And professionalism, which I think is an important substitute but one that needs a little clarification. When we think of professionalism we may think of competence, but there's more to it than that. Professionalism has a virtuous aspect. For example, there's a commitment to exemplary practice. Professionals don't need anybody to check on them, to push them, to lead them. They are compelled from within.

This interview with Tom Sergiovanni by Ron Brandt is from *Educational Leadership*. February 1992, Vol. 49, No. 5, pp. 46–49. Reprinted by permission.

But surely the leader—the official leader—helps develop such qualities?
You're saying you need leadership to get the substitutes for leadership. You may be right.

But another way to get at it is to change the metaphor for the school. We view schools as formal organizations, so we think of leadership in terms of the hierarchical Bureaucracy. In communities, on the other hand, people are bonded together in different ways, and a different kind of authority compels them to behave as they do.

I think we've had it upside down. Traditionally we've served our leaders. I'm suggesting that in an idea-based organization, a community enterprise, if you will see, I still slip and use words like "organization"—the person with moral authority is cast in the role of serving the enterprise even more than others who also serve the enterprise.

That doesn't mean you're a weak leader, that you don't hold people accountable. You can express disappointment. You can talk about letting standards fall. As a matter of fact, I talk about leadership by outrage. In traditional management, when you base your leadership on bureaucratic authority, you're supposed to be cold and calculating. When you base it on psychological authority, you have to be sensitive to the interpersonal needs of other people, which might mean treating them like children, I don't know. But when you base it on moral authority, you can behave normally. You can get angry and be disappointed, just as you do outside your official role, even with loved ones. When you treat people that way, it seems to me, you're treating them much more authentically.

Now, obviously, you're not going to be harsh and cruel. But if you're not pleased with something I did, say so. If I let the standard down, it's a learning experience for me, an opportunity for me to renew my commitment. And not only should leaders practice leadership by outrage but they should encourage it in others. Nobody has a special license to protect the standard. The only thing that makes the leader special is that she or he is a better follower: better at articulating the purposes of the community; more passionate about them, more willing to take time to pursue them.

This is a very different way to think about leadership. What caused you to reexamine your ideas?
Well, frankly, much of my work in leadership over the years has been more part of the problem than the solution. When I recognized that,

I began to rethink traditional management theory. It came about gradually, of course, but I particularly remember doing a workshop on leadership styles somewhere in the Philippines. We had an instrument and so on, and I would say that to be effective in a certain situation the leader should do such and such. And every time I'd say that, one person would ask, "What do you mean by effective?" He was a pain in the neck for the whole two days, so I put him down and ignored him—but that has haunted me ever since.

I began to feel that what I had been saying was vacuous, that everything I had been advocating about leadership was all process, no substance.

About 1980 or so I suffered what you might call a professional mid-life crisis, feeling that many of the things that had been important to me—my work on motivation and so on—now seemed devoid of meaning.

So I began a different line of inquiry. About 1982 or 1983, it became clear to me that while my students and people in workshops were patient and respectful of what I had to say, they actually made a distinction between workshop knowledge and real life career knowledge. In real life, they weren't driven by the theories I taught them but by other ideas and other conceptions. They even had different theories about how the world worked. So I began to get curious about what kinds of theories principals, superintendents, and other leaders had in their heads—why they thought the way they did.

Well, I began to discover that they were not uncomfortable with ideas like moral authority. Maybe they wouldn't use the same words I would, but they were concerned about things like school pride, and they continued to do things like copying materials for teachers or putting kids' clothes in a washing machine and washing them. There's nothing in the literature that says principals ought to do that, and yet those are powerful moral statements.

So that led to my doing a series of studies on leadership. What I began to understand was that ideas were the key. Leadership wasn't just coming up with a slogan that you could call your "vision"; these leaders brought to their faculties a set of conceptions that became an idea structure for their schools. These idea structures weren't necessarily the same—some were even quite different from what I would have liked—but in each case there was something this person believed in and felt passionately about; it was that person's source of authority.

As I continued to think about it, the critical theorists—writers like William Foster and Richard Bates—helped me understand why I was beginning to have misgivings about psychologically based theory, including my own earlier work on motivation, going way back to my dissertation. For example, for the most part, Maslow and Herzberg didn't study females, so they espoused motivational theories that had to do with achievement and competitiveness; they didn't think about caring and nurturing relationships. And the work of McClelland provided us with a male model of achievement that focused on internal criteria for excellence and individual success rather than on community building.

By the way, that was another shocker for me, because when I first began to read the feminist literature, I thought, "Who are these arrogant people?" But it turns out they were right. Management literature traditionally was written by men for men, and its values—individualism, competition—define success in a masculine way. Maslow's theory exults self-actualization: self this, self that. Well, as a group, women tend not to define success and achievement that way. They are more concerned with community and sharing.

Some men might say defensively that what you're saying is sexist; that it replaces men's belief that theirs is the better way with a view that women's way is superior.

Well, I don't have hard evidence, but you don't need hard evidence to make informed judgments. My reading of the literature on successful schools shows that while women are underrepresented in principalships, they are overrepresented in successful principalships, so there may be something to it.

You're not saying that men can't learn this?

Absolutely not.

But the most telling argument against an emphasis on process rather than substance is that a person can be successful in a psychological sense but the enterprise may not get better. As a matter of fact, it could get worse, because people who have no moral commitment but all the leadership skills can be very skillful in promoting the wrong things. We'd be better off if they weren't such good leaders.

As you reexamine leadership, are you questioning the concept of instructional leadership?

Sorry, yes. Nobody defends bureaucratic authority; they all see that as "command" leadership. Some have a problem with my criticisms of psychologically based leadership, because leadership style, personality, motivation—all that stuff—seem to be at the core of what we study. But where others really part company with me is when I say that technical rationality is not a very good source of authority either!

What do you mean by technical rationality?

I mean the findings from the teaching effectiveness research, school effectiveness research, and so on. I realize that some people won't like what I'm saying, because we've been led to believe that that stuff is terrific. But there's a strong case for teachers needing to create their practice in use—for not treating the research on teaching as a set of prescriptions. It doesn't tell you what to do, it informs your practice.

That may be true, but I wouldn't define instructional leadership in those terms. To me, it simply means that the principal is deeply interested in and knowledgeable about teaching and learning.

Well, I have problems even with that. I may have been influenced too much by what I've seen happen in Texas. In 1984, Texas passed a law declaring that all of its principals would be instructional leaders. It required that they all take 36 hours of instruction on something called "the lesson cycle," and that they learn how to use the Texas teacher appraisal system. They were to go into teachers' classrooms at least four times a year and make sure the teachers were teaching the "proper way." I think the term "instructional leadership" has been captured; it's been spoiled.

And, anyhow, surely there are better labels. How about principal teacher? At least principal teacher suggests a kind of community with teachers. Instructional leader suggests that others have got to be followers. The legitimate instructional leaders, if we have to have them, ought to be teachers. And principals ought to be leaders of leaders: people who develop the instructional leadership in their teachers.

So much for principal leadership. We're hearing more and more about teacher leadership these days. Where's the overlap?
I think you worry less about leadership if you think that one of the challenges of leadership is to establish substitutes for it. The more successful we are at establishing substitutes for leadership, the less important it becomes to worry about who are leaders and who aren't.

What does this mean in practice? Suppose I'm a school principal. What do I do?
Well, there's no easy recipe. I suppose it requires a change in your own mindscape about how human enterprises work. They're much more loosely connected than they appear. Can I use social science jargon as a shortcut? Traditional management theory is based on the notion that organizations are managerially tight and culturally loose when it's probably the opposite: they are managerially loose.

For example, evaluation systems don't matter a nickel. They're one of the biggest wastes of time in the world, because it's not important what a person does the two times that you're in the classroom observing him or her. When you're not there, teachers teach in ways that make sense to them according to the norms. And norms are connected not to the managerial side of life but to the cultural side. So we need to acknowledge that and try to figure out how we can develop a "stickier" management and leadership practice, one that touches people and stays with them.

You can't abandon hierarchical leadership entirely, can you?
No, there are five sources of authority, not three. You've still got bureaucratic, psychological, and technical-rational—but competence and virtue should dominate, I think; the other three should supplement. You fall back on hierarchical authority and psychological leadership because the world is imperfect. But if you're really a professional—there's something antithetical, isn't there, between the notions of professionalism and leadership?

Is there?
Yes. The more leadership is emphasized, the less professionalism flourishes.

In a particular school community?
Yes, and the inverse tends to be true. The more professionalism is thriving, the less need there is for leadership.

So it's no accident that at a time we're beginning to stress teacher professionalism—
I think the door is open now to a kind of revolution. We're beginning to recognize that schools are special places where people care about teaching and learning. They're not like most organizations; you can't apply organizational principles to places characterized by sandboxes, books, and children. Schools are more like families and small communities where, if you can develop the right substitutes, you can throw traditional leadership away. There's no need for it ever again.

About the Interviewer: Ron Brandt, retired, is a former Executive Director of the Association for Supervision and Curriculum Development.

Section 1

Leadership as a
Moral Craft

What makes a good leader? That's a tough question. Context plays a key role in deciding whether certain approaches to leadership will be effective or not. Thus what a leader says and does to be effective in one kind of enterprise may not lead to effectiveness in another kind of enterprise. Susan Moore Johnson puts it this way: "Leadership looks different—and is different—depending on whether it is experienced in a legislature, on a battlefield, at a rally, on a factory floor, or in a school district." (1996, 14)

Schools need special leadership because schools are special places. Sure schools share with other enterprises common managerial requirements that insure basic levels of organizational purpose, competence, reliability, structure and stability. But schools must respond as well to the unique political realities they face. After all, schools belong to parents and children, interact with the needs of local businesses, churches and other community groups, and have a unique relationship with state governments. These "stakeholders" don't always agree and it takes a high level of political skill for school leaders to bring about the necessary consensus and commitment to make schools work well for everyone.

Schools also need special leadership because they are staffed by professionals who don't react warmly to the kind of hierarchically based command leadership or hero leadership that characterizes so many other kinds of organizations. Nor do these professionals have a high tolerance for bureaucratic rituals. Though school leaders may be in charge, the best of them are aware that often the teachers they supervise know more about what needs to be done and particularly how to do it than they do. This reality creates large ability-authority gaps in schools that must be breached.

Schools are places where children and young people struggle to achieve the necessary developmental growth and to accumulate the necessary intellectual knowledge, practical skills, habits of mind and character traits that will enable them to "run the country" in just a few short years after they graduate from high school. The presence of children and young adults in a learning and developing environment and the awesome responsibility that schools have to serve these students well are still other characteristics that make schools unique and that require us to view school leadership differently. Ordinary images of how to organize, provide leadership and support, motivate, and ensure accountability just don't seem to fit schools very well.

The unique context for schooling, particularly in a democratic society, raises the question of sources of authority for leadership practice. As important as a school leader's personality and interpersonal skills may be to success, and as handy as bureaucratic reasons may be to use, neither are sufficiently powerful to provide that leader with the sources of authority needed to reach students, parents, teachers and others in powerful ways. Needed are substitutes for bureaucratic and personal leadership that compel people to respond to internal reasons. Substitutes for leadership are exactly what a moral emphasis in leadership can provide.

The articles included in Section 1 describe a new kind of leadership that I believe must become the framework for the way we do things in schools. This leadership is moral because it emphasizes the bringing together of diverse people into a common cause by struggling to make the school a covenantal community. Covenantal communities have at their center shared ideas, principles, and purposes that provide a powerful source of authority for leadership practice. In covenantal communities the purpose of leadership is to create a shared followership. Leaders in covenantal communities function as head followers.

The language of head followership focuses attention on what is being followed. There can be no leadership if there is nothing important to follow. Leadership, in this sense, is more cognitive than interpersonal and the source of authority for leadership practice is based on goals, purposes, values, commitments and other ideas that provide the basis for followership. This idea based leadership is much more likely to motivate people to action than is interpersonally based leadership. The evidence for this assertion can be found in your own personal experiences.

Imagine a leader who you personally admire because of her or his ability to handle people well. But you do not agree with this person's goals. Compare this leader with another who you may not even like very much but whose ideas make a great deal of sense to you.

Which of the two leaders would you be more willing to follow? This scenario illustrates the four pillars of leadership: leaders, followers, ideas, and action. All four are needed for leadership to be effective. Leadership that does not result in action, for example, is like a work only half completed no matter how eloquent its ideas or passionate its followers. Action is much more likely to result when leaders and followers are connected to each other by a commitment to common ideas.

In the first article "Leadership and Excellence in Schooling" I describe five forces that leaders can use to bring about or to preserve changes needed to improve schooling. The forces are technical, human, educational, symbolic and cultural. Though all five are important and can contribute to the development of a moral basis for leadership it is the symbolic and cultural that wind up being the most powerful.

"Administration as a Moral Craft," the second article, is an edited chapter from *The Principalship: A Reflective Practice Perspective*. This reading shows how successful principals bring together the heart, head and hand of leadership in their practice. The moral nature of administrative work in schools is then discussed and the idea of leaders cultivating a culture of followership is developed. This article shows how successful schools are also schools of character, examines how our democratic traditions relate to moral leadership and concludes with a discussion of purposing as a key function of school leadership.

Viewing leadership as a moral craft reminds us of the powerful roles that the inner characteristics of leadership play in bringing about successful schooling. Though school leaders must be many things to many people and school leaders must pay attention to educational, management and political roles, at the heart of their work they are ministers. *Minister,* after all, is the root word in administer. Whatever else principals do they must first minister to the purposes of the school, minister to the idea structure that provides a source of authority for what people do, and minister to the needs of those who day by day do the work of the school. The remaining articles in Section I expand on these themes by providing examples of how moral leadership works and what principals and other school leaders can do to make it work effectively in their own schools.

Moral leadership is the means that principals and others can use to build connections. As students, teachers, parents, and administrators are more firmly connected to themselves, each other, their work and their responsibilities higher levels of academic and civic engagement will be observed. This engagement provides the framework for improving student performance as well as levels of civility, increasing the quality of parental participation, and enhancing teacher professionalism.

REFERENCE

Johnson, Susan Moore. (1996). *Leading to change.* San Francisco, CA: Jossey-Bass Publishers.

Leadership and Excellence in Schooling

Excellent schools need freedom within boundaries.

by Thomas J. Sergiovanni

> It is in and through symbols that man, consciously or unconsciously, lives, works and has his meaning.—Thomas Carlyle

Is your school a good school? When Joan Lipsitz posed this question to principals of the excellent middle schools she studied, she found that they had difficulty defining what made their schools special or what the dimensions of excellence in schooling were. "You will have to come and see my school," was the typical response.[1]

Excellence is readily recognized in our ordinary experiences. It is difficult to put our finger on what makes a particular athletic or artistic performance excellent. But we know excellence when we see it. The earmarks of an excellent piano performance may be found not in the notes played but in the pauses between them. Clearly, excellence is multidimensional, holistic.

Competence, by contrast, is marked by mastery of certain predetermined, essential fundamentals. The piano student achieves mastery and thus is able to play the notes flawlessly and deliver a performance recognized as technically competent.

Similarly, we know excellent schools when we experience them, despite difficulties in definition. In excellent schools things "hang together"; a sense of purpose rallies people to a common cause; work

"Leadership and Excellence in Schooling" by Thomas J. Sergiovanni is reprinted from *Educational Leadership,* February, 1984, vol. 41, no. 5, pp. 4–13 by permission from ASCD. All rights reserved.

has meaning and life is significant; teachers and students work together and with spirit; and accomplishments are readily recognized. To say excellent schools have high morale or have students who achieve high test scores or are schools that send more students to college misses the point. Excellence is all of these and more.

EXCELLENCE, NOT COMPETENCE

Should we expect more from our schools than the satisfaction of knowing they're performing "up to standard" and that students are competent performers? Most surveys indicate that basic skill learning and developing fundamental academic competence—the indicators of effectiveness common to the school effectiveness literature—are paramount goals in the minds of most parents and teachers. But, pushed a bit further, parents and teachers provide a more expansive view of excellence, which includes developing a love of learning, critical thinking and problem-solving skills, aesthetic appreciation, curiosity and creativity, interpersonal competence, and so on. Parents want a complete education for their children. Indeed our society requires it. Our young need to become cultured, educated citizens able to participate fully in society, not just trained workers with limited potential for such participation.

> **To say excellent schools . . . have students who achieve high test scores . . . misses the point.**

Important differences exist among incompetent, competent, and excellent schools and their leaders. Schools managed by incompetent leaders simply don't get the job done. Typically, such schools are characterized by confusion and inefficiency in operation and malaise in human climate. Student achievement is lower in such schools. Teachers may not be giving a fair day's work for a fair day's pay. Student absenteeism, discipline, and violence may be a problem. Conflict may characterize interpersonal relationships among faculty or between faculty and supervisors. Parents may feel isolated from the school. Competent schools, by contrast, measure up to these and other standards of effectiveness. They get the job done in a satisfactory manner. Excellent schools, however, exceed the expectations necessary to be considered satisfactory. Students in such schools accomplish far more and teachers work much harder than can ordinarily be expected.

LEADERSHIP FORCES AND EXCELLENCE

Leadership has several aspects, each of which contributes uniquely to school competence and to school excellence. The current focus in leadership theory and practice provides a limited view, dwelling excessively on some aspects of leadership to the virtual exclusion of others. Unfortunately, these neglected aspects of leadership are linked to excellence—a revelation now unfolding from recent research on school effectiveness and school excellence.

Aspects of leadership can be described metaphorically as forces available to administrators, supervisors, and teachers as they influence the events of schooling. Force is the strength or energy brought to bear on a situation to start or stop motion or change. Leadership forces can be thought of as the means available to administrators, supervisors, and teachers to bring about or preserve changes needed to improve schooling.

At least five leadership forces can be identified:

- *Technical*—derived from sound management techniques
- *Human*—derived from harnessing available social and interpersonal resources
- *Educational*—derived from expert knowledge about matters of education and schooling
- *Symbolic*—derived from focusing the attention of others on matters of importance to the school
- *Cultural*—derived from building a unique school culture.

The first two forces have dominated the leadership literature in recent years and loom large in training programs offered through ASCD's National Curriculum Study Institutes.

1. *The technical leader assumes the role of "management engineer."* By emphasizing such concepts as planning and time management technologies, contingency leadership theories, and organizational structures, the leader provides planning, organizing, coordinating, and scheduling to the life of the school. An accomplished management engineer is skilled at manipulating strategies and situations to ensure optimum effectiveness.

2. *The human leader assumes the role of "human engineer."* By emphasizing such concepts as human relations, interpersonal competence, and instrumental motivational technologies, she or he pro-

vides support, encouragement, and growth opportunities to the school's human organization. The skilled engineer is adept at building and maintaining morale and using such processes as participatory decision making.

3. *The educational leader assumes the role of "clinical practitioner," bringing expert professional knowledge and bearing as they relate to teaching effectiveness, educational program development, and clinical supervision.* The clinical practitioner is adept at diagnosing educational problems; counseling teachers; providing for supervision, evaluation, and staff development; and developing curriculum. One wonders how such essential concerns of *school* leadership could, for so long, have been neglected in the literature of educational administration.

In an earlier era the *educational* aspects of leadership were center stage in the literature of educational administration and supervision. Principals were considered to be instructional leaders, and an emphasis on schooling characterized university training programs. However, advances of management and social science theory in educational administration and supervision soon brought to center stage technical and human aspects. John Goodlad has been a persistent critic of the displacement of educational aspects of leadership in favor of technical and human. He argues, "But to put these matters at the center, often for understandable reasons of survival and expediency, is to commit a fundamental error which ultimately, will have a negative impact on both education and one's own career. *Our work, for which we will be held accountable, is to maintain, justify, and articulate sound, comprehensive programs of instruction for children and youth.*"[2]

He states further, "It is now time to put the right things at the center again. And the right things have to do with assuring comprehensive, quality educational programs in each and every school under our jurisdiction."[3]

The technical, human, and educational forces of leadership, brought together in an effort to maintain or improve schooling, provide the critical mass needed for competent schooling. A deficit in any one of the three upsets this critical mass, and less effective schooling is likely to occur. Recent studies of excellence in organizations suggest that despite the link between these three aspects of leadership and competence in schooling, their presence does not guarantee excellence. Excellent organizations, schools among them, are characterized by other leadership qualities; forces described here as symbolic and cultural.

4. *The symbolic leader assumes the role of "chief" and by empha-sizing selective attention (the modeling of important goals and behav-iors) signals to others what is of importance and value.* Touring the school; visiting classrooms; seeking out and visibly spending time with students; downplaying management concerns in favor of educational ones; presiding over ceremonies, rituals, and other important occasions; and providing a unified vision of the school through proper use of works and actions are examples of leader activities associated with this fourth force.

Purposing is of major concern to the symbolic force. Peter Vaill defines purposing as "that continuous stream of actions by an organization's formal leadership which has the effect of inducing clarity, consensus, and commitment regarding the organization's basic purposes."[4] Students and teachers alike want to know what is of value to the school and its leadership; desire a sense of order and direction; and enjoy sharing this sense with others. They respond to these conditions with increased work motivation and commitment.

Of less concern to the symbolic force is the leader's behavioral style. Instead, what the leader stands for and communicates to others is emphasized. The object of symbolic leadership is the stirring of human consciousness, the integration and enhancing of meaning, the articulation of key cultural strands that identify the substance of a school, and the linking of persons involved in the school's activities to them. As Lou Pondy suggests "What kind of insights can we get if we say that the effectiveness of a leader lies in his ability to make activity meaningful for those in his role set—not to change behavior but to give others a sense of understanding what they are doing, and especially to articulate it so they can communicate about the mean-ing of their behavior?"[5] Providing meaning and rallying people to a common cause constitute effectiveness in symbolic leadership.

Leaders typically express symbolic aspects of leadership by work-ing beneath the surface of events and activities and searching for deeper meaning and value. As Robert J. Starratt suggests, leaders seek to identify the roots of meaning and the flow and ebb of daily life in schools so that they might provide students, teachers, and members of the community with a sense of importance, vision, and purpose about the seemingly ordinary and mundane. Indeed, these leaders bring to the school a sense of drama in human life that permits persons to rise above the daily routine. They are able to see the significance of what a group is doing, and indeed could be doing. They have a feel for the dramatic possibilities inherent in most situations and are able to urge people to go beyond the routine, to break out of the mold into something more lively and vibrant. And finally, symbolic leaders are able to communicate their sense of vision by words and examples. They use easily understood language symbols, which communicate a sense of excitement, originality, and freshness. These efforts provide opportunities for others in the school to experience this vision and to obtain a sense of purpose so that they might come to share in the ownership of the school enterprise more fully.[6]

Warren Bennis argues that a compelling vision is the key ingredient of leadership in the excellent organizations he studied. Vision refers to the capacity to create and communicate a view of a desired state of affairs that induces commitment among those working in the organization.[7] Vision, then, becomes the substance of what is communicated as symbolic aspects of leadership are emphasized.

5. *The cultural leader assumes the role of "high priest," seeking to define, strengthen, and articulate those enduring values, beliefs, and cultural strands that give the school its unique identity.* As high priest the leader is engaged in legacy building, and in creating, nurturing, and teaching an organizational saga,[8] which defines the school as a distinct entity within an identifiable culture. The words clan or tribe come to mind. Leader activities associated with the cultural force include articulating school purposes and mission; socializing new members to the culture; telling stories and maintaining or reinforcing myths, traditions, and beliefs; explaining "the way things operate around here"; developing and displaying a system of symbols over time; and rewarding those who reflect this culture.

The net effect of the cultural force of leadership is to bond together students, teachers, and others as believers in the work of the school. Indeed, the school and its purposes are somewhat revered as if they resembled an ideological system dedicated to a sacred mission. As persons become members of this strong and binding culture, they are provided with opportunities for enjoying a special sense of personal importance and significance. Their work and their lives take on a new importance, one characterized by richer meanings, an expanded sense of identity, and a feeling of belonging to something special—all highly motivating conditions.[9]

Before further pursuing the powerful forces of symbolic and cultural leadership, let's view the five forces in the form of a leadership hierarchy as depicted in Figure 1. The following assertions can be made about the relationships of these forces:

1. Technical and human leadership forces are generic and thus share identical qualities with competent management and leadership wherever they are expressed. They are not, therefore, unique to the school and its enterprise regardless of how important they may be.

2. Educational, symbolic, and cultural leadership forces are situational and contextual, deriving their unique qualities from specific matters of education and schooling. These qualities differentiate educational leadership, supervision, and administration from management and leadership in general.

3. Technical, human, and educational aspects of educational leadership forces are essential to competent schooling, and their absence contributes to ineffectiveness. The strength of their presence alone, however, is not sufficient to bring about excellence in schooling.

4. Cultural and symbolic aspects of substantive leadership forces are essential to excellence in schooling. Their absence, however, does not appear to negatively affect routine competence.

5. The greater the presence of a leadership force higher in the hierarchy, the less important (beyond some unknown minimum presence) are others below.

CULTURE AND PURPOSE: ESSENTIALS OF EXCELLENCE

Culture building and practicing the art of purposing are the essentials of symbolic and cultural leadership forces. Culture can be described as the collective programming of the mind that distinguishes the members of one school from another.[10] Cultural life in schools is constructed reality, and leaders play a key role in building this reality. School culture includes values, symbols, beliefs, and shared meanings of parents, students, teachers, and others conceived as a group or community. Culture governs what is of worth for this group and how members should think, feel, and behave. The "stuff" of culture includes a school's customs and traditions; historical accounts; stated and unstated understandings; habits, norms, and expectations; common meanings and shared assumptions. The more understood, accepted, and cohesive the culture of a school, the better able it is to move in concert toward ideals it holds and objectives it wishes to pursue.

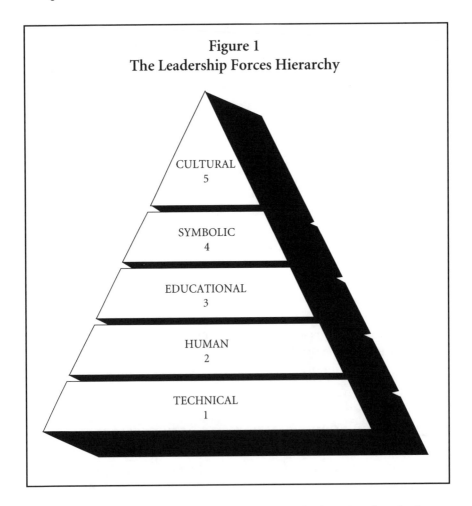

Figure 1
The Leadership Forces Hierarchy

CULTURAL
5

SYMBOLIC
4

EDUCATIONAL
3

HUMAN
2

TECHNICAL
1

All schools have cultures: strong or weak, functional or dysfunctional. Successful schools seem to have strong and functional cultures aligned with a vision of excellence in schooling. This culture serves as a compass setting to steer people in a common direction; provides a set of norms that defines what people should accomplish and how; and provides a source of meaning and significance for teachers, students, administrators, and others as they work. Strong, functional cultures are domesticated in the sense that they emerge deliberately— they are nurtured and built by the school leadership and membership.

Weak cultures, by contrast, result in a malaise in schools characterized by a lack of understanding of what is to be accomplished and a lack of excitement for accomplishment itself. Sometimes cultures are strong and dysfunctional. In this case, students may have banded together to build a strong culture directed at disrupting the school or coercing other students to misbehave or perform poorly. Teachers, too, can be sources of problems in strong, dysfunctional cultures if they place their own interests first. In some schools, for example, an informal culture may exist with strong norms that dictate to faculty how they should behave. It might be unacceptable, for example, for teachers to take work home with them or to visit with students after school. Teachers who are working very hard might be considered as "eager beavers" or "rate busters," and as a result find themselves distanced from this culture. Cultures of this sort might be referred to as wild. Wild cultures are not in control of administrators, supervisors, parents, teachers, and students as a cohesive group. They develop more informally or willy-nilly. When a dysfunctional wild culture exists in a school, excellence requires the building of a new, strong culture.

> When a dysfunctional wild culture exists in a school, excellence requires the building of a new, strong culture.

Culture building requires school leaders to give more attention to the informal, subtle, and symbolic aspects of school life. Teachers, parents, and students need answers to some basic questions: What is the school about? What is important here? What do we believe in? Why do we function the way we do? How are we unique? How do I fit into the scheme of things? Answering such questions provides an orderliness to one's school life derived from a sense of purpose and enriched meanings.

"The task of leadership is to create the moral order that binds them—and the people around them," notes Thomas B. Greenfield.[11]

James Quinn states, "The role of the leader, then, is one of orchestrator and labeler: taking what can be gotten in the way of action and shaping it—generally after the fact—into lasting commitment to a new strategic direction. In short, he makes meanings."[12]

Leadership as culture building is not a new idea, but one solidly imbedded in our history and well known to successful school and other leaders. In 1957, Philip Selznick wrote:

The art of the creative leader is the art of institution building, the reworking of human and technological materials to fashion an organism that embodies new and enduring values. . . . To institutionalize is to infuse with value beyond the technical requirements of the task at hand. The prizing of social machinery beyond its technical role is largely a reflection of the unique way it fulfills personal or group needs. Whenever individuals become attached to an organization or a way of doing things as persons rather than as technicians, the result is a prizing of the device for its own sake. From the standpoint of the committed person, the organization is changed from an expendable tool into a valued source of personal satisfaction. . . . The institutional leader, then, is primarily an expert in the promotion and protection of values.[13]

And in 1938, the noted theorist, Chester Barnard, stated the following about executive functions:

The essential functions are, first to provide the system of communications; second, to promote the securing of essential efforts; and third, to formulate and define purpose. . . . It has already been made clear that, strictly speaking, purpose is defined more nearly by the aggregate of action taken than by any formulation in words.[14]

FREEDOM WITH RESTRICTIONS

Excellent schools have central zones composed of values and beliefs that take on sacred or cultural characteristics. Indeed, it might be useful to think of them as having an official "religion," which gives meaning and guides appropriate actions. As repositories of values, these central zones become sources of identity for teachers and students, giving meaning to their school lives. The focus of leadership, then, is on developing and nurturing these central zone patterns so that they provide a normative basis for action within the school.

In some respects, the concept of central zone suggests that effective schools are tightly structured. That is, they are organized in a highly disciplined fashion around a set of core ideas, which spell out the way of life in the school and govern behaviors. This is in contrast to recent developments in organizational theory which describe schools as being loosely structured entities. James G. March, a noted organizational theorist, speaks of educational organizations as being organized anarchies.[15] Similarly, Karl Weick uses the phrase loose coupling to describe the ways in which schools are organized.[16]

Indeed Weick believes that one of the reasons for ineffectiveness in schooling is that schools are managed with the wrong theory in mind.

Contemporary thought, Weick argues, assumes that schools are characterized by four properties: the existence of a self-correcting rational system among people who work in a highly interdependent way; consensus on goals and the means to obtain these goals; coordination by the dissemination of information; and predictability of problems and responses to these problems. In fact, he notes, none of these properties are true characteristics of schools and how they function. Effective school administrators in loosely coupled schools, he observes, need to make full use of symbol management to tie together the system. In his words:

> People need to be part of sensible projects. Their action becomes richer, more confident, and more satisfying when it is linked with important underlying themes, values and movements. . . . Administrators must be attentive to the 'glue' that holds loosely coupled systems together because such forms are just barely systems.[17]

Weick continues:

> The administrator who manages symbols does not just sit in his or her office mouthing clever slogans. Eloquence must be disseminated. And since channels are unpredictable, administrators must get out of the office and spend lots of time one on one—both to remind people of central visions and to assist them in applying these visions to their own activities. The administrator teaches people to interpret what they are doing in a common language.[18]

Recent observations about the school effectiveness literature point out that effective schools are not loosely coupled or structured at all but instead are tightly coupled.[19] My interpretation of the school effectiveness excellence literature leads me to believe that these schools are both tightly coupled and loosely coupled, an observation noted as well by Peters and Waterman in their studies of America's best-run cooperations. There exists in excellent schools a strong culture and a clear sense of purpose, which defines the general thrust and nature of life for their inhabitants. At the same time, a great deal of freedom is given to teachers and others as to how these essential core values are to be honored and realized. This combination of tight structure around clear and explicit themes, which represent the core of the school's culture, and of autonomy for people to pursue these themes in ways that make sense to them, may well be a key reason for their success.

Figure 2
The Forces of Leadership and Excellence in Schooling

Force	Leadership Role Metaphor	Theoretical Constructs	Examples	Reactions	Link to Excellence
1. Technical	"Management engineer"	• Planning and time management technologies • Contingency leadership theories • Organizational structure	• Plan, organize coordinate, and schedule • Manipulate strategies and situations to ensure optimum optimum effectiveness	People are managed as objects of a mechanical system. They react to efficient management with indifference but have a low tolerance for inefficient management.	Presence is important to achieve and maintain routined school competence but not sufficient to achieve excellence. Absence results in school ineffectiveness and poor morale.
2. Human	"Human engineer"	• Human relation supervision • "Linking" motivation theories • Interpersonal competence • Conflict management • Group cohesiveness	• Provide needed support • Encourage growth and creativity • Build and maintain morale • Use participatory decision making	People achieve high satisfaction of their interpersonal needs. They like the leader and the school and respond with positive interpersonal behavior. A pleasant atmosphere exists that facilitates the work of the school.	
3. Educational	"Clinical practitioner"	• Professional knowledge and bearing • Teaching effectiveness • Educational program design • Clinical supervision	• Diagnose educational problems • Counsel teachers • Provide supervision and evaluation • Provide inservice • Develop curriculum	People respond positively to the strong expert power of the leader and are motivated to work. They appreciate the assistance and concern provided.	Presence is essential to routine competence. Strongly linked to, but still not sufficient for, excellence in schooling. Absence results in ineffectiveness.
4. Symbolic	"Chief"	• Selective attention • Purposing • Modeling	• Tour the school • Visit classrooms • Know students • Preside over ceremonies and rituals	People learn what is of value to the leader and school, have a sense of order and direction and enjoy sharing that sense with others. They respond increased with motivation and commitment.	Presence is essential to excellence in schooling through absence does
5. Cultural	"High priest"	• Climate, clan, culture • Tightly structured values—loosely structured system • Ideology • "Bonding" motivion theory	• Articulate school purpose and mission • Socialize new members • Tell stories and maintain reinforcing myths • Explain SOPs • Define uniqueness • Develop and display a reinforcing symbol system • Reward those who reflect the culture	People become believers in the school as an ideological system. They are members of a strong culture that provides them with a sense of personal importance and significance and work meaningfulness which is highly motivating.	not appear to negatively impact routine competence.

The combination of tight structure and loose structure corresponds very well to three important human characteristics associated with motivation: commitment, enthusiasm, and loyalty to school. Teachers, students, and other school staff need to:

1. Find their work and personal lives meaningful, purposeful, sensible, and significant

2. Have some reasonable control over their work activities and affairs and to be able to exert reasonable influence over work events and circumstances

3. Experience success, think of themselves as winners, and receive recognition for their success.

People are willing to make a significant investment of time, talent, and energy in exchange for enhancement and fulfillment of these three needs.[20]

LEADERSHIP DENSITY

Figure 2 provides a summary of the relationship between the five forces of leadership and excellence in schooling. Included for each force are the dominant metaphor for leadership role and behavior; important theoretical constructs from which such behavior is derived; examples of the behaviors in school leadership; reactions of teachers and others to the articulation of leadership forces; and links of each force to school competence and excellence.

As leaders are able to better understand and incorporate each of the five forces, they must be prepared to accept some additional burdens. Symbolic and cultural forces are very powerful influences of human thought and behavior. People respond to these forces by bonding together into a highly normative-cohesive group, and this group in turn bonds itself to the school culture in an almost irrational way. The "cult" metaphor communicates well the nature and effect of extremely strong bonding. How strong is the bonding of excellent schools? Is it possible that there are limits beyond which bonding works against excellence? As bonding grows, one is apt to "think" less and "feel" more about work and commitments to school.

No easy answer exists to this problem. But the burdens of leadership will be less if leadership functions and roles are shared and if the concept of leadership density were to emerge as a viable replacement for principal leadership. The moral and ethical foundation for leadership will be strengthened if leaders place outer world concerns (such as the welfare of schooling) before inner concerns for self-expression and personal success. Leaders might select as their slogan Kant's admonition, "Act so that you treat humanity, whether in your own person or in that of another, always as an end and never as a means only."

NOTES

1. Joan Lipsitz, *Successful Schools for Young Adolescents* (New Brunswick, NJ: Transaction Books, 1983). (Available from the Center for Early Adolescence at the University of North Carolina-Chapel Hill in Carrboro, NC).

2. John Goodlad, "Educational Leadership: Toward the Third Era," *Educational Leadership* 35, (January 1978): 326.

3. Ibid., p. 331.

4. Peter B. Vaill, "The Purposing of High Performing Systems," in *Leadership and Organizational Culture,* eds., Thomas J. Sergiovanni and John E. Corbally (Urbana-Champaign: University of Illinois Press, 1984).

5. Louis Pondy, "Leadership Is a Language Game," in *Leadership Where Else Can We Go?* eds., Morgan W. McCall, Jr., and Michael M. Lombardo (Durham, NC: Duke University Press, 1978), p. 94.

6. See, for example, his "Apostolic Leadership," Jesuit Commission on Research and Development, San Jose, CA, June, 1977 (available from the Commission of Fordham University, Lincoln Center, New York, NY); and "Contemporary Talk on Leadership: Too Many Kings in the Parade?" *Notre Dame Journal of Education 4,* 1 (1973).

7. Warren Bennis, "Transformation Power and Leadership" in T.J. Sergiovanni and J.E. Corbally, op. cit.

8. Burton R. Clark, "The Organizational Saga in Higher Education," *Administrative Science Quarterly* 17, 2 (1972).

9. See, for example, Thomas J. Peters and Robert H. Waterman, Jr., In Search of Excellence •NY: Harper & Row, 1982), particularly Chapter 4; and T.J. Sergiovanni, "Motivation to Work, Satisfaction and Quality of Life in Schools," *Issues in Education: A Forum of Research and Opinion* 1, 2 (1984).

10. G. Hofstede, *Cultures Consequences* (Beverly Hills: Sage Publications, 1980), p. 13.

11. Thomas B. Greenfield, "Leaders and Schools: Willfulness and Non-Natural Order in Organization," in T.J. Sergiovanni and J.E. Corbally, op. cit.

12. James B. Quinn, "Formulating Strategy One Step at a Time," *Journal of Business Strategy* (Winter 1981): 59.

13. Philip Selznick, *Leadership and Administration: A Sociological Interpretation* (NY: Harper & Row, 1957).

14. Chester I. Barnard. *The Functions of the Executive.* Cambridge, Mass.: Harvard University Press, 1968, p. vii.

15. Michael D. Cohen, James G. March, and Johan Olson, "A Garbage Can Model of Organizational Choice," *Administrative Science Quarterly* 17, 1 (1972): 1–25.

16. Karl E. Weick, "Administering Education in Loosely Coupled Schools," *Phi Delta Kappan* 27, 2 (June 1982): 673-676.

17. Ibid., p. 675

18. Ibid., p. 676

19. See, for example, Michael Cohen, "Instructional Management and Social Conditions in Effective Schools," in *School Finance and School Improvement: Linkages in the 1980's,* eds. Allan Odden and L. Dean Webb. 1983 Yearbook of the American Educational Finance Association.

20. See, for example, Peters and Waterman, op. cit.; Sergiovanni, op. cit.; and J. Richard Hackman and Greg R. Oldham, *Work Redesign* (Reading, Mass.: Addison-Wesley, 1980).

Administering as a Moral Craft

by Thomas J. Sergiovanni

THE PRINCIPALSHIP: A REFLECTIVE PRACTICE PERSPECTIVE

In the book a number of conceptions of the principal have been discussed: Strategic problem solver, cultural leader, barterer, and initiator are examples. It's fair to ask whether these are the roles and images of leadership that one should follow in order to be an effective principal. The answer is yes—well, no—actually maybe. Similarly, what about the motivational concepts and ideas, the new principles of management and leadership, the characteristics of successful schools, the forces of leadership, strategies for bringing about change, and the dimensions of school culture discussed in other chapters? Will these ideas, if routinely applied, help one to be an effective principal? The answer is the same. Yes—well, no—actually maybe. Unfortunately there is no guarantee that the concepts presented [here] will fit all readers or the contexts and problems they face in the same way. Leadership is a personal thing. It comprises three important dimensions—one's heart, head, and hand.

THE HEART, HEAD, AND HAND OF LEADERSHIP

The *heart* of leadership has to do with what a person believes, values, dreams about, and is committed to—that person's *personal vision,* to use a popular term. To be sure, sharing personal conceptions of what is a good school will reveal many common qualities, but what often makes them personal statements is that they will differ as well. The *head* of leadership has to do with the theories of practice each of us

This article is an edited version of Chapter 15, "Administering as a Moral Craft," from *The Principalship: A Reflective Practice Perspective,* Third Edition. Boston: Allyn and Bacon, 1995, pp. 307–321. Adapted by permission of the publisher.

has developed over time and our ability to reflect on the situations we face in light of these theories. This process of reflection combined with our personal vision becomes the basis for our strategies and actions. Finally, the *hand* of leadership has to do with the actions we take, the decisions we make, the leadership and management behaviors we use as our strategies become institutionalized in the form of school programs, policies, and procedures. As with heart and head, how we choose to manage and lead are personal reflections not only of our vision and practical theories but of our personalities and our responses to the unique situations we face as well. In this idiosyncratic world, one-best-way approaches and cookie cutter strategies do not work very well. Instead, diversity will likely be the norm as principals practice. Each principal must find her or his way, develop her or his approach if the heart, head, and hand of leadership are to come together in the form of successful principalship practice.

In this idiosyncratic world, one-best-way approaches and cookie cutter strategies do not work very well.

Does that mean that the concepts presented in this book are not true? If they are not truths to be emulated and imitated, what are they? They comprise a different kind of truth. They represent a concept boutique on one hand and a metaphor repository on another. The idea is to visit the boutique trying on one idea after another seeking a fit here or there and to visit the repository seeking to create new understandings of situations one faces and new alternatives to one's practice. As boutique and repository the role of knowledge about schooling changes from being something that principals apply uniformly to being something useful that informs the decisions they make as they practice. This is the nature of reflective practice.

THE MORAL IMPERATIVE

Although many may prefer the work of administration to be some sort of an applied science that is directly connected to a firm knowledge base of theory and research, the reality we face is that it is much more craftlike. The message from this reality is equally clear. Successful practice requires the development of craft know-how. Craft know-how according to Blumberg (1989) includes the following:

- Being able to develop and refine "a nose for things."
- Having a sense of what constitutes an acceptable result in any particular problematic situation.
- Understanding the nature of the "materials" with which one is working. This includes oneself as a "material" that needs to be understood, as well as others. It also includes understanding the way other parts of the environment may affect the materials and the acceptableness of the solution at a particular point in time.
- Knowing administrative techniques and having the skill to employ them in the most efficacious way possible.
- Knowing what to do and when to do it. This involves not only pragmatic decisions—what behavior or procedure is called for at a particular time—but also implies issues of right and wrong. Much as Tom's (1984) description of teaching is that of a "moral" craft, so too is the practice of administration one in which there are moral dimensions to every action taken, with the possible exception of those that are simply mundane. This is not to suggest that administrators are aware of these moral dimensions at all times; it is simply to suggest that they are present.
- Having a sense of "process," that is, being able to diagnose and interpret the meaning of what is occurring as people interact in any problematic situation. (47)

Yet, administering schools, as Blumberg suggests, is no ordinary craft. Bringing together head, heart, and hand in practice; the unique nature of the school's mission; and the typically loosely structured, nonlinear, and messy context of schooling combine to make administering a *moral* craft, a fate shared with teaching (Tom, 1984) and supervision (Sergiovanni and Starratt, 1988). The reasons for this moral imperative are as follows:

1. The job of the principal is to transform the school from being an organization of technical functions in pursuit of objective outcomes into an *institution*. Organizations are little more than technical instruments for achieving objectives. As instruments they celebrate the value of effectiveness and efficiency by being more concerned with "doing things right" than with "doing right things." Institutions, however, are effective and efficient and more. They are responsive, adaptive enterprises that exist not only to get a particular job done but as entities in and of themselves. As Selznick (1957)

points out, organizations become institutions when they transcend the technical requirements needed for the task at hand. In his words, "Institutionalization is a *process*. It is something that happens to an organization over time, reflecting the organization's own distinctive history, the people who have been in it, the groups it embodies and the vested interests they have created, and the way it has adopted to its environment. . . ." (Selznick, 1957:16). He continues:

> Organizations become institutions as they are infused with value, that is, prized not as tools alone but as sources of direct personal gratification and vehicles of group integrity. This infusion produces a distinct identity for the organization. Where institutionalization is well advanced, distinctive outlooks, habits, and other commitments are unified, coloring all aspects of organizational life and lending it a social integration that goes well beyond formal coordination and command. (Selznick, 1954:40)

Selznick's conception of institution is similar to the more familiar conception of school as *learning community*. To become either, the school must move beyond concerns for goals and roles to the task of building purposes into its structure and embodying these purposes in everything that it does with the effect of transforming school members from neutral participants to committed followers. The embodiment of purpose and the development of followership are inescapably moral.

2. The job of the school is to transform its students not only by providing them with knowledge and skills but by building *character* and instilling *virtue*. As Cuban (1988) points out, both technical and moral images are present in teaching and administering. "The technical image contains values that prize accumulated knowledge, efficiency, orderliness, productivity, and social usefulness; the moral image, while not disregarding such values, prizes values directed at molding character, shaping attitudes, and producing a virtuous, thoughtful person" (xvii). Technical and moral images of administration cannot be separated in practice. Every technical decision has moral implications. Emphasizing orderliness, for example, might serve as a lesson in diligence for students and might be a reminder to teachers that professional goals cannot be pursued to the extent that bureaucratic values are compromised.

3. Whether concern is for virtue or efficiency, some *standard* has to be adopted. What is efficient in this circumstance? How will virtue be determined? Determining criteria for effective teaching, deciding

on what is a good discipline policy, or coming to grips with promotion criteria standards, for example, all require value judgments. Answers to questions of how and what cannot be resolved objectively as if they were factual assertions, but must be treated as normative assertions. Normative assertions are true only because we decide that they are. "We must decide what ought to be the case. We cannot *discover* what ought to be the case by investigating what is the case" (Taylor, 1961:248). Normative assertions are moral statements.

4. Despite commitments to empowerment and shared decision making, relationships between principals and others are inherently unequal. Although often downplayed, and whether they want it or not, principals typically have more *power* than teachers, students, parents, and others. This power is in part derived legally from their hierarchical position, but for the most part it is obtained de facto by virtue of the greater access to information and people that their position affords them. They are not chained to a tight schedule. They do a lot of walking around. They are the ones who get the phone calls, who are out in the streets, who visit the central office, who have access to the files, and so forth. As a result they function more frequently in the roles of figurehead and liaison with outside agencies. They have greater access to information than do other people in the school. This allows them to decide what information will be shared with others, what information will be withheld, and frequently what information will be forgotten. Often teachers and others in the school rely on the principal to serve as the "coordinating mechanism" that links together what they are doing with what others are doing. In teaching, where much of the work is invisible, the coordinating function is a powerful one. Furthermore, much of the information that principals accumulate is confidential. When teachers have problems they frequently confide in the principal. Information is a source of power, and the accumulation of power has moral consequences.

Whenever there is an unequal distribution of power between two people, the relationship becomes a moral one. Whether intended or not, leadership involves an offer to control. The follower accepts this offer on the assumption that control will not be exploited. In this sense, leadership is not a right but a responsibility. Morally speaking, its purpose is not to enhance the leader's position or make it easier for the leader to get what she or he wants but to benefit the school. The test of moral leadership under these conditions is whether the competence, well-being, and independence of the follower are enhanced as a result of accepting control and whether the school benefits. Tom (1980) makes a similar argument in pointing out that "the teacher-student relationship is inherently moral because of its inequality" (317).

5. The context for administration is surprisingly loose, chaotic and ambiguous. Thus, despite demands and constraints that circumscribe the principal's world, in actuality, *discretion* is built into the job, and this discretion has moral implications.

For example, frequently how things look is different than how things work. In their research on the reality of managing schools. Morris and colleagues (1984) discovered numerous instances in which principals and schools were able to develop implicit policies and pursue courses of action that only remotely resembled officially sanctioned policies and actions. They noted that not only maintaining student enrollment levels but increasing them was often viewed as a managerial necessity by principals. However, they were not motivated for official "educational" or "societal" reasons, but to protect or enhance the resource allocation base of their schools. Staffing patterns and budget allocations were often linked to a principal's standing among peers and were related as well to morale and productivity levels among teachers. Furthermore, principals of larger schools had more clout with the central office. Simply put, more staff and bigger budgets were viewed as being better. Schools losing resources, however, "usually suffer a decline in purposefulness, security, and confidence that goes beyond the loss of operating funds" (128).

As a result, principals tended to view monitoring, protecting, and increasing school enrollments and attendance as one of their key, albeit implicit, tasks. This led them to engage in courses of action that were at variance with the officially sanctioned definition of their tasks and roles. There was, for example, a concerted effort to change existing programs and revise the existing curriculum so they were more attractive to students and thus better able to hold their enrollment. One of the principals reported, "We may have to cut physics, for instance, and add environmental science. It's in. . . . I've got to get my faculty to see that they have to reshape the traditional curriculum of the school. Their jobs are at stake" (Morris et al., 1984:128-129). Another principal in their study worked to change his school's kindergarten program so that it was more structured and "rigorous," not for educational reasons or philosophical commitments but so that the school would be better able to compete with the neighborhood Catholic school.

Despite clear guidelines governing attendance procedures (e.g., fixed attendance boundaries and age requirements), principals became flexible by bending the rules for student admissions and taking liberties with reporting enrollment information to the central office. In the words of one principal, "In general, I'm not picky about where the students in the school live," noting further that if a child subsequently became a behavioral problem or was suspected of being a behavioral problem she always checked the home address (Morris et al., 1984:30). Some principals were inclined to look the other way even when they knew that students came from other school districts if they thought the students were "extremely bright." Some principals used leniency in enforcing attendance boundaries as the lever to extract better behavior and more achievement form students. Principals stressed that they were doing the parents and students a favor and expected good behavior in return. Not all students were treated equally. While bright students were encouraged to attend, "troublemakers" were not. In the words of one principal, "Let him go, that guy's been nothing but trouble for us" (Morris et al., 1984:131).

> **Although discretion can provide principals with a license for abuse, it is also a necessary prerequisite for leadership.**

Although discretion can provide principals with a license for abuse, it is also a necessary prerequisite for leadership. "From choice comes autonomy. Autonomy is the necessary condition for leadership to arise. Without choice, there is no autonomy. Without autonomy, there is no leadership" (Cuban, 1988: xxii). Discretion, therefore, is necessary if principals are to function effectively. Yet, how principals handle discretion raises moral issues and has moral consequences for the school.

NORMATIVE RATIONALITY

Key to understanding the moral dimension in leadership is understanding the difference between *normative rationality* (rationality base on what we believe and what we consider to be good) and *technical rationality* (rationality based on what is effective and efficient). Happily, the two are not mutually exclusive. Principals want what is good and what is effective for their schools, but when the two are in conflict, the moral choice is to prize the former over the latter. Starratt makes the point poignantly as follows: "'Organizational effectiveness' employs technical rationality, functional rationality, linear logic. Efficiency is the highest value, not loyalty, harmony, honor, beauty, truth. One can run an efficient extermination camp or an efficient monastery. The principles of efficiency are basically the same in either context" (Sergiovanni and Starratt, 1988:218).

Normative rationality provides the basis for moral leadership. Instead of just relying on bureaucratic authority to force a person to do something or a psychological authority to manipulate a person into doing something, the leader—principal or teacher as the case may be—provides reasons for selecting one alternative over another. The reasons are open to discussion and evaluation by everyone. To pass the test of normative rationality, the reasons must embody the purposes and values that the group shares—the sacred covenant that bonds everyone in the school together as members of a learning community.

Normative rationality influences the practice of leadership in schools in two ways. Principals bring to their job biases and preju- dices, ways of thinking, personality quirks, notions of what works and what doesn't, and other factors that function as personal theories of practice governing what they are likely to do and not do, and school cultures are defined by a similar set of biases that represent the center of shared values and commitments that define the school as an institution. Both are sources of norms that function as standards and guidelines for what goes on in the school. As a school's culture is strengthened and its center of values becomes more public and per- vasive, normative rationality becomes more legitimate. Everyone knows what the school stands for and why and can articulate these purposes and use them as guidelines for action. This in-building of purpose "involves transforming [persons] in groups from neutral, technical units into participants who have a peculiar stamp, sensitiv- ity, and commitment" (Selznick, 1957:150).

FOLLOWERSHIP IS THE GOAL

The importance of purposing changes how leadership is understood and practiced. With purposing in place in a school, one cannot become a leader without first becoming a follower. What it means to be a follower and what it means to be a subordinate are very different. Subordinates respond to bureaucratic authority and sometimes to personal authority. Followers, by contrast, respond to ideas. You can't be a follower unless you have something to follow. Furthermore, as Zaleznik (1989) suggests, subordinates may cooperate with the management system but are rarely committed to it. By contrast, one of the hallmarks of being a follower is commitment. As Kelly (1988) points out, followers "are committed to the organization and to a purpose, principle, or person outside themselves. . . ..[And as a result] they build their competence and focus their efforts for maximum impact" (144). Followers, by definition, are never constrained by minimums but are carried by their commitment to performance that typically exceeds expectations. Subordinates, by contrast, do what they are supposed to; they tend not to do more.

> Subordinates respond to bureaucratic authority and sometimes to personal authority. Followers, by contrast, respond to ideas.

When subordinateness is transcended by followership, a different kind of hierarchy emerges in the school. Principals, teachers, students, parents, and others find themselves equally "subordinate" to a set of ideas and shared conceptions to which they are committed. As a result, teachers respond and comply not because of the principal's directives but out of a sense of obligation and commitment to these shared values. That's what it means to be a follower.

The principal's job is to provide the kind of purposing to the school that helps followership to emerge. She or he then provides the conditions and support that allow people to function in ways that are consistent with agreed-upon values. At the same time, the principal has a special responsibility to continually highlight the values, to protect them, and to see that they are enforced. The true test of leadership under these conditions is the principal's ability to get others in the school to share in the responsibility for guarding these values.

One of the persistent problems of leadership is obtaining compliance, which is at the heart of the principal's role. Invariably, compliance occurs in response to some sort of authority, but not all sources of authority are equally powerful or palatable. In this book, four sources of authority have been described: bureaucratic, personal, professional, and moral. All four have a role to play if schools are to function effectively, however, the four compete with each other.

When principals use bureaucratic authority, they rely on rules, mandates, and regulations in efforts to direct thought and action. When principals use personal authority, they rely on their own interpersonal style, cleverness, guile, political know-how, and other forms of managerial and psychological skill in order to direct thought and action. When principals rely on professional authority, they appeal to expertness, expecting everyone to be subordinate to a form of technical rationality that is presumably validated by craft notions of what constitutes best educational practice or scientific findings from educational research. When principals rely on moral authority, they bring to the forefront a form of normative rationality as discussed above that places everyone subordinate to a set of ideas, ideals, and shared values and asks them to respond morally by doing their duty, meeting their obligations, and accepting their responsibilities. All are important, but the art of leadership is balancing the four competing sources of authority in such a way that moral and professional authority flourish without neglecting bureaucratic and personal authority.

> ... for the school to transform itself into an institution, a learning community must emerge.

THE CHALLENGE OF LEADERSHIP

In the principalship, the challenge of leadership is to make peace with two competing imperatives, the managerial and the moral. The two imperatives are unavoidable and the neglect of either creates problems. Schools must be run effectively and efficiently if they are to survive. Policies must be in place. Budgets must be set. Teachers must be assigned. Classes must be scheduled. Reports must be completed. Standardized tests must be given. Supplies must be purchased. The school must be kept clean. Students must be protected from violence. Classrooms must be orderly. These are essential tasks that guarantee the survival of the school as an organization. Yet, for the school to transform itself into an institution, a learning community must emerge. Institutionalization is the moral imperative that principals face.

Discussing the moral imperative in administration; proposing such leadership values as purposing, empowerment, outrage, and kindling outrage in others; and arguing for the kind of balance among bureaucratic, psychological, professional, and moral sources of authority in schools that noticeably tilts toward professional and moral challenge the "professional manager" conception of the principalship by placing concerns for substance firmly over concerns for process.

On the upside, the development of school administration as a form of management technology brought with it much needed attention to the development of better management know-how and of organizational skills badly needed to deal with an educational system that continues to grow in technical, legal, and bureaucratic complexity. On the downside, professionalism has too often resulted in principals thinking of themselves less as statespersons, educators, and philosophers, and more as organizational experts who have become absorbed in what Abraham Zaleznik (1989) refers to as the *managerial mystique.* "As it evolved in practice, the mystique required managers to dedicate themselves to process, structures, roles, and indirect forms of communication and to ignore ideas, people, emotions, and direct talk. It deflected attention from the realities [of education] while it reassured and rewarded those who believed in the mystique" (2). The managerial mystique holds so strongly to the belief that "the right methods" will produce good results that the methods themselves too often become surrogates for results, and to the belief that management and bureaucratic controls will overcome human shortcomings and enhance human productivity that controls become ends in themselves. School improvement plans, for example, become substitutes for school improvements; scores on teacher appraisal forms become substitutes for good teaching; accumulating credits earned in courses and required inservice workshops become substitutes for changes in school practice; discipline plans become substitutes for student control; leadership styles become substitutes for purpose and substance; congeniality becomes a substitute for collegiality; cooperation becomes a substitute for commitment; and compliance becomes a substitute for results.

Zaleznik (1989) maintains that the managerial mystique is the antithesis of leadership. The epitome of the managerial mystique is the belief that anyone who can manage one kind of enterprise can also manage any other kind. It is the generic management techniques and generic interpersonal skills that count rather than issues of purpose and substance. Without purpose and substance, Zaleznik argues, there can be no leadership. "Leadership is based on a compact that binds those who lead and those who follow into the same moral, intellectual and emotional commitment" (15).

BUILDING THE CHARACTER OF YOUR SCHOOL

One of the major themes [presented here] is the importance of the school's culture. For better or for worse, culture influences much of what is thought, said, and done in a school. Character is a concept similar to culture but much less neutral. A school's character is known by how the school is viewed by members and outsiders in ethical and moral terms. Building and enhancing the school's character is the key to establishing its credibility among students, teachers, parents, and administrators and externally in the broader community. Wilkins (1989) notes that the components of an organization's character are its common understandings of purpose and identity that provide a sense of "who we are"; faith of members in the fairness of the leadership and in the ability of the organization to meet its commitments and to get the job done; and the distinctive cultural attributes that define the tacit customs, networks of individuals, and accepted ways of working together and of working with others outside of the organization. How reliable are the actions of the school? How firm is the school in its convictions? How just is its disposition? Wilkins points out that purpose, faith, and cultural attributes "add up to the collective organizational competence" (1989:27). To him, faith is a particularly important component of an organization's character, and loss of faith in either the organization or its leadership results in loss of character. Building faith restores character. Enhancing faith increases character. Without faith and character the organization and its members are not able to move beyond the ordinary to extraordinary performance. Without tending to the moral imperative there can be no organizational character, and without character a school can be neither good nor effective for very long.

> For better or for worse, culture influences much of what is thought, said, and done in a school.

A COMMITMENT TO DEMOCRATIC VALUES

The inescapable moral nature of administrative work and in particular seeking to establish moral authority embodied in the form of purposing and shared values and expressed as "cultural leadership" raises important questions of manipulation and control. Cultural leadership can provide principals with levers to manipulate others that are more powerful than levers associated with bureaucratic and psychological authority. Lakomski (1985) raises the question squarely:

> To put the objection more strongly, it may be argued that if all cultural analysis does is to help those in power, such as principals and teachers, to oppress some students more effectively by learning about their views, opinions, and 'student cultures', then this method is just another and more sophisticated way to prevent students (and other oppressed groups) from democratic participation in educational affairs (15).

Her comments apply as well to teachers and others. Furthermore, cultural leadership can become a powerful weapon for masking the many problems of diversity, justice, and equality that confront schools. There is nothing inherently democratic about cultural leadership, and indeed, depending on its substance this kind of leadership can compromise democratic values. Consensus building and commitment to shared values can often be little more than devices for maintaining an unsatisfactory status quo and for discouraging dissent. Finally, not all covenants are equal. The values that define the "center" of different school communities are not interchangeable.

Cultural leadership can be understood and practiced as a technology available to achieve any goal and to embody any vision or as a means to celebrate a particular set of basic values that emerge from the American democratic tradition. It makes a difference, for example, whether the basic values that define a school community revolve around themes of efficiency, effectiveness, and excellence or whether these are considered to be mere means values in service to such ends values as justice, diversity, equality, and goodness. In the spirit of the latter point of view, Clark and Meloy (1984) propose the Declaration of Independence as a metaphor for managing schools to replace bureaucracy. This metaphor guarantees to all persons that school management decisions will support such values as equality, life, liberty, and the pursuit of happiness based on the consent of the governed.

Discussion of democracy in schools typically wins nods from readers. However, as Quantz, Cambron-McCabe, and Dantley (1991) point out, democracy is not always understood as both process and substance.

There is often a confusion of democracy with pure process—the belief that as long as there is some form of participatory decision-making that democracy has been achieved. We argue, however, that democracy implies both a process and a goal, that two, while often contradictory, cannot be separated. We believe that democratic processes cannot justify undemocratic ends. For example, we cannot justify racial and gender inequity on the basis that the majority voted for it. While this dual-reference test for democracy is not simple or clean, while it often requires us to choose between two incompatible choices, both in the name of democracy, we can conceive of no other way to approach it. In other words, even though an appeal to democratic authority cannot provide a clear and unequivocable blueprint for action in every particular instance, it can provide a general and viable direction for intelligent and moral decision-making by school administrators.

One of the challenges of moral leadership in schools is to engage oneself and others in the process of decision making without thought to self-interest. Can we discuss and decide our grading policies, discipline procedures, student grouping practices, supervisory strategies, and so forth without regard to whether we will be winners or loser? Sending children routinely to the principal's office for discipline, for example, or favoring homogeneous grouping of students may be in the interest of teachers but not students. Requiring all teachers to teach the same way may make it easier for the principal to hold teachers accountable, but not for teachers who want to teach in ways that make sense to them. Discouraging parental involvement in school governance makes for fewer headaches for school people but disenfranchises the parents. What is just under these circumstances? John Rawls (1971) has suggested that decisions such as these should be made by people choosing in a hypothetical position of fairness under what he called "a veil of ignorance." The idea is to pretend that we don't know anything about ourselves—our sex, our race, our position in the school, our talents, and so forth. We don't know, in other words, whether we are black or white, principal or teacher, student or custodian, parent or teacher aide. Our identities are only revealed when the veil of ignorance is lifted. Rawls maintains that in this way we are likely to fashion our principles and make decisions regardless of who we turn out to be. With bias diminished, chances are that the principles would be fairer and the decisions more just.

Exhibit 1
Job Commitment Index

Responses: 4–Strongly Agree, 3–Agree, 2–Disagree, 1–Strongly Disagree

		1	2	3	4
1.	Most of the important things that happen to me involve my work.	—	—	—	—
2.	I spend a great deal of time on matters related to my job, both during and after hours.	—	—	—	—
3.	I feel badly if I don't perform well on my job.	—	—	—	—
4.	I think about my job even when I'm not working.	—	—	—	—
5.	I would probably keep working even if I didn't have to.	—	—	—	—
6.	I have a perspective on my job that does not let it interfere with other aspects of my life.	—	—	—	—
7.	Performing well on my job is extremely important to me.	—	—	—	—
8.	Most things in my life are more important to me than my job.	—	—	—	—
9.	I avoid taking on extra duties and responsibilities in my work.	—	—	—	—
10.	I enjoy my work more than anything else I do.	—	—	—	—
11.	I stay overtime to finish a job even if I don't have to.	—	—	—	—
12.	Sometimes I lie awake thinking about the next day's work.	—	—	—	—
13.	I am able to use abilities I value in doing my job.	—	—	—	—
14.	I feel depressed when my job does not go well.	—	—	—	—
15.	I feel good when I perform my job well.	—	—	—	—
16.	I would not work at my job if I didn't have to.	—	—	—	—

A PERSONAL NOTE

How committed are you to becoming a successful school principal? Generally speaking, commitment to your present job provides a good idea of one's overall commitment to work. For an indication of your present job commitment, respond on the Job Commitment Scale Exhibit 1. This scale contains 16 items about how people feel about their jobs. Indicate the extent to which you agree or disagree with each item. As you count your score, reverse-score items 6, 8, and 16. Your score will range from a low of 16 to a high of 64, with 64 representing the highest level of commitment. Keep in mind that there is always the chance that a person's commitment to work may be high, but that her or his present job presents such unusual difficulties that low commitment and a low score result.

In his studies of high-performing leaders, Peter Vaill (1984) found that "(1) Leaders of high-performing systems put in extraordinary amounts of time; (2) Leaders of high-performing systems have very strong *feelings* about the attachment of the system's purposes; and (3) Leaders of high-performing systems focus on key issues and variables" (94). Vaill notes that "there are of course many nuances, subtleties, and local specialists connected with the leadership of many high-performing systems, but over and over again, Time, Feeling, and Focus appear no matter what else appears" (94). The three go hand in hand. Vaill states, for example, that administrators who put in large amounts of time without feeling or focus are exhibiting "workaholism." Time and feeling without focus, however, often lead to dissipated energy and disappointment. Finally, time and focus without feeling seem to lack the necessary passion and excitement for providing symbolic and cultural leadership. Successful leaders—principals among them—are not afraid of hard work. By putting in large amounts of time, they demonstrate that they are not afraid of hard work; however, they don't dissipate this time by taking on everything. Instead, they concentrate their efforts on those characteristics and values that are clearly more important to the success of their organization than are others. Furthermore, unlike cold, calculated, objective, and uninvolved managers, they bring to their enterprises a certain passion that affects others deeply.

As a result of his extensive studies of the principalship and school leadership, William Greenfield (1985) concludes that principals need to be more passionate about their work, clearer about what they seek to accomplish, and more aggressive in searching for understandings that lead to improved schooling. Greenfield speaks of passion as "believing in the worth of what one seeks to accomplish and exhibiting in one's daily action a commitment to the realization of those goals and purposes" (17). He maintains that clarity about goals and outcomes should be accompanied by a commitment to flexibility regarding processes, procedures, and other means to attain ends.

Finally, anyone who is aspiring to be a good principal needs to have some sense of what she or he values, something to be committed to, a compass to help navigate the way—a personal vision. As Roland Barth (1990) points out,

> Observers in schools have concluded that the lives of teachers, principals, and students are characterized by brevity, fragmentation, and variety. During an average day, for instance, a teacher or principal engages in several hundred interactions. So do many parents. A personal vision provides a framework with which to respond and to make use of the many prescriptions and conceptions of others. But more important, these ideas centered around schools as communities of learners and leaders have provided me with a road map which has enabled me to respond to the hundreds of daily situations in schools—in a less random and more thoughtful way. Without a vision, I think our behavior becomes reflexive, inconsistent, and shortsighted as we seek the action that will most quickly put out the fire so we can get on with putting out the next one. In five years, if we're lucky, our school might be fire free—but it won't have changed much. Anxiety will remain high, humor low, and leadership muddled. Or as one teacher put it in a powerful piece of writing, "Without a clear sense of purpose we get lost, and our activities in a school become but empty vessels of our discontent." Seafaring folk put it differently: "For the sailor without a destination, there is no favorable wind." (211)

One of the great secrets of leadership is that before one can command the respect and followership of others, she or he must demonstrate devotion to the organization's purposes and commitment to those in the organization who work day by day on the ordinary tasks that are necessary for those purposes to be realized. As Greenleaf (1977) points out, people "will freely respond only to individuals who are chosen as leaders because they are proven and trusted as servants" (10). This perspective has come to be known as servant leadership (Greenleaf, 1977), with its basic tenets found in the biblical verse: "Ye know that rulers of the Gentiles lorded over them, and that their great ones exercised authority over them. Not so shall it be among you: but whosoever would become great among you shall be your minister and whosoever would be first among you shall be your servant" (Matthew 20:25).

Servant leadership describes well what it means to be a principal. Principals are responsible for "ministering" to the needs of the schools they serve. The needs are defined by the shared values and purposes of the school's covenant. They minister by furnishing help and being of service to parents, teachers, and students. They minister by providing leadership in a way that encourages others to be leaders in their own right. They minister by highlighting and protecting the values of the school. The principal as minister is one who is devoted to a cause, mission, or set of ideas and accepts the duty and obligation to serve this cause. Ultimately her or his success is known by the quality of the followership that emerges. Quality of followership is a barometer that indicates the extent to which moral authority has replaced bureaucratic and psychological authority. When moral authority drives leadership practice, the principal is at the same time a leader of leaders, follower of ideas, minister of values, and servant to the followership.

REFERENCES

Barth, Roland S. 1990. *Improving Schools from Within*. San Francisco: Jossey-Bass.

Blumberg, Arthur. 1989. *School Administration as a Craft*. Boston: Allyn and Bacon.

Clark, David L., and Judith M. Meloy. 1984. "Renouncing Bureaucracy: A Democratic Structure for Leadership in Schools," in T.J. Sergiovanni and J.H. Moore, eds., *Schooling for Tomorrow: Directing Reforms to Issues that Count*. Boston: Allyn and Bacon.

Cuban, Larry. 1988. *The Managerial Imperative and the Practice of Leadership in Schools*. Albany: State University of New York Press.

Greenfield, William D. 1985. "Instructional Leadership: Muddles, Puzzles, and Promises." Athens: The Doyne M. Smith Lecture, University of Georgia, June 29.

Greenleaf, Robert K. 1977. *Teacher as Servant*. New York: Paulist Press.

Kelly, Robert E. 1988. "In Praise of Followers," *Harvard Business Review* (Nov.-Dec.).

Lakomski, Gabriele. 1985. "The Cultural Perspective in Educational Administration," in R.J.S. Macpherson and Helen M. Sungaila, eds., *Ways and Means of Research in Educational Administration*. Armidale, New South Wales: University of New England.

Morris, Van Cleave, Robert L. Crowson, Cynthia Porter-Gehrie, and Emanual Hurwitz, Jr. 1984. *Principals in Action*, Columbus, OH: Merrill.

Peters, Tom, and Nancy Austin. 1985. *A Passion for Excellence.* New York: Random House.

Quantz, Richard A., Nelda Cambron-McCabe, and Michael Dantley. 1991. "Preparing School Administrators for Democratic Authority: A Critical Approach to Graduate Education." *The Urban Review,* 23(1), 3–19.

Rawls, John. 1971. *A Theory of Justice.* Cambridge, MA: Harvard University Press.

Selznick, Philip. 1957. *Leadership in Administration: A Sociological Interpretation.* New York: Harper & Row. California Paperwork Edition 1984. Berkeley: University of California Press.

Sergiovanni, Thomas J., and Robert J. Starratt. 1988. *Supervision: Human Perspectives.* New York: McGraw-Hill.

Smith, John K., and Joseph Blasé. 1987. "Educational Leadership as a Moral Concept." Washington, DC: American Educational Research Association.

Taylor, Paul W. 1961. *Normative Discourse.* Englewood Cliffs, NJ: Prentice-Hall.

Tom, Alan. 1980. "Teaching as a Moral Craft: A Metaphor for Teaching and Teacher Education," *Curriculum Inquiry* 10(3).

Tom, Alan. 1984. *Teaching as a Moral Craft.* New York: Longman.

Vaill, Peter B. 1984. "The Purposing of High-Performing Systems," in Thomas J. Sergiovanni and John E. Corbally, eds., *Leadership and Organizational Culture.* Urbana-Champaign: University of Illinois Press.

Wilkins, Alan L. 1989. *Developing Corporate Character.* San Francisco: Jossey-Bass.

Zaleznik, Abraham. 1989. *The Managerial Mystique Restoring Leadership in Business.* New York: Harper & Row.

New Sources of Leadership Authority

by Thomas J. Sergiovanni

I n academic circles the topic of leadership represents one of social science's greatest disappointments. As recently as 1985, for example, Warren Bennis and Burt Nanus (1985) pointed out that despite the thousands of studies of leaders conducted in the last seventy-five years we still do not understand what distinguishes leaders from nonleaders, effective leaders from ineffective leaders, and effective organization from in-effective organizations. They join a chorus of other social scientists and management theorists who have lost faith in traditional conceptions of leadership.

There are, I believe, two reasons for the failure of leadership as academic discipline. First, we have come to view leadership as behavior rather than action, as something psychological rather than spiritual, as having to do with persons rather than ideas. And second, in trying to understand what drives leadership we have overemphasized bureaucratic, psychological, and technical-rational authority, seriously neglecting professional and moral authority. In the first reason we have separated the hand of leadership from the head and the heart, and the second reason we have separated the process of leadership from it substance. The result has been a leadership literature that borders on being vacuous and a leadership practice that is based on this literature that may not be leadership at all. These are harsh words not spoken lightly.

The bright side of the picture is that in our schools a practice of leadership is emerging that requires us to redefine the concept. The

"New Sources of Leadership" by Thomas J. Sergiovanni is from Marshall Saskin and Herbert J. Walberg: *Educational Leadership and School Culture.* Copyright 1993 by McCutchan Publishing Corporation, Berkeley, CA 94702. Permission granted by the publisher.

field is ahead of the theory and as a result, we have a literature and an official conversation about leadership that does not account enough for successful leadership practice. To reflect emerging practice we have to move the moral dimension in leadership from the periphery to the center of inquiry, discussion, and practice.

OFFICIAL AND UNOFFICIAL VALUES OF MANAGEMENT

Moving the moral dimension of leadership to the center of practice forces us to rethink some widely accepted assumptions about the values that undergird school management theory. We can group values into three major categories: those that compute the official values of management, those that are not fully recognized (semi-official), and those that are unofficial. The three categories are illustrated below:

Figure 1
The Values That Undergird School Management Theory

Official Values	*Semi-Official Values*	*Unofficial Values*
Secular authority (I have faith in the authority of the bureaucratic system.)	**Sense experience** (I have faith in my experiences.)	**Sacred authority** (I have faith in the authority of the community, in professional norms, in school norms, and in ideals.)
Science (I have faith in empirical findings.)	**Intuition** (I have faith in my insight.)	**Emotions** (I have faith in my feelings.)
Deductive logic (I have faith in deductive reasoning.)		

All of the values are legitimate. But in today's practice sacred authority and emotions are neglected and often ignored. When acknowledged, they are often thought to be weak, impressionistic, and feminine concepts. Sense experience and intuition, though acknowledged, do not enjoy equal standing with secular authority, science, and deductive logic. Failure to give equal attention to all of the values leads to impoverished theories of school management and leadership.

How do the values influence practice? Secular authority, science, and deductive logic provide scripts for leaders and others to follow. They rely on technical-rational knowledge that is considered to be more important than the personal knowledge of leaders. Teachers, principals, and superintendents are expected to be subordinate to this knowledge. As a result, discretion is reduced—even eliminated. Without discretion school administrators are not free to decide—they can only do; they are not free to write the script of schools—they can only follow the script that is provided. But without discretion there can be no real leadership.

> Secular authority, science, and deductive logic provide scripts for leaders and others to follow.

In recent years sense experience and intuition have made some important inroads in becoming legitimate values of management. The work on reflective practice within the professions is one noteworthy example. This work makes a distinction between scientific knowledge and professional knowledge, claiming that the latter is created in use as professionals solve problems too unique for standard recipes. It suggests that the traditional ways of knowing—secular authority, science, and deductive logic—should inform the decisions that administrators make but should not prescribe their practice. Knowing, it is claimed, is in the action itself as professionals research the context and experiment with different courses of action. Sense experience and intuition have wide currency among practicing school administrators.

Sacred authority and emotion seem also to enjoy wide currency among many school administrators. From the two come such practices as purposing and building a covenant of shared values that bond people together in a common cause and such practice goals as transforming schools from organizations to communities. Hunter Lewis (1990) believes that the operational value systems based on sacred authority and emotion are actually more alike than different. They share, in his view, three features. First, they emphasize the building of group identities an cohesion that make people feel special. Second, they promote a distinct way of life or way of organizing society that provides people with an emotional identity. The third feature, according to Lewis, is that they all require an emotional stimulus such as a mission, a sense of purpose, a covenant of shared values that represents the core or center defining the group as a community. Lewis refers to these value systems as "systems of blood."

> **Giving more credence to sense experience and intuition and accepting sacred authority and emotion allow for a new kind of leadership— one based on moral authority.**

Giving more credence to sense experience and intuition and accepting sacred authority and emotion allow for a new kind of leadership—one based on moral authority. Morally based leadership transforms schools from ordinary organizations to communities. This transformation can inspire the kind of commitment, devotion, and service that will make our schools unequaled among society's institutions. But how do we know if this new leadership will work? The answer lies in the extent to which it is able to tap the human will in a fashion that both motivates and inspires.

WHAT MOTIVATES, WHAT INSPIRES?

When I recently asked Catherine Piersall, principal of the San Antonio School in Dade City, Florida, about what kinds of events and circumstances in a typical school day made her feel especially good and what kinds made her feel lousy, she responded: "The positive feedback and 'evidence' of successful decisions make me feel especially good. For example, watching a new program, a new approach, a new teacher, and seeing this situation as being successful is very rewarding to me. Another example of something that makes me feel good is to hear good reports on 'my' students who have left our school and are doing well in other school or life situations. The phone call or comment from a parent who tells me that 'Johnny had such problems that year at San An, but thanks to your help he's doing great now." I feel lousy as a result of the inability to do what I think needs to be done to help a child; the inability to control the situations that lead to inappropriate behavior, learning problems, and the like." It's hard to find any hint of self-interest in her response or that he emotions do not count as she assesses her situation. Nor does Piersall respond as a freestanding individual separate from her commitments to the school and to other groups with which she identifies. Is she an anomaly? Would we have any reason to believe that what matters to her is different from what matters to her teachers or what matters to principals and teachers elsewhere?

From most leadership theory today we would conclude that Catherine Piersall is indeed an anomaly. My research, however, leads me to conclude otherwise. Most current leadership is based on a theory of motivation that has overplayed the importance of self-interest, personal pleasure, and individual choice as the driving forces for what we do. Underplayed are the more altruistic reasons for doing things and the extent to which we identify with and are influenced by membership groups (such as church, ethnic groups, the teaching profession, school, social networks, neighborhood, nation). The consequence has been a practice that underestimates the complexity of human nature and the capacity of people to be motivated for reasons other than self-interest. We lead with the wrong assumptions in mind. And as a result, the yield in commitment and performance is well under that which most teachers are able to give and want to give to their work. This situation will not improve by trying harder to do the same things, by fine-tuning present leadership practices. Improving our yield means changing our outlook.

> **Improving our yield means changing our outlook.**

Traditional leadership theory assumes that we are driven by a desire to maximize self-interest and thus we continually calculate the costs and benefits of our options, choosing those that either make us winners or keep us from losing. Self-interest is so dominant in this thinking that emotions such as love, loyalty, outrage, obligation, duty, goodness, dedication, and desire to help count very little in determining what we do and why do what we do. Emotions are no more than currency that one uses to get something. Within this view, for example, a loving relationship is considered to be little more than a contract within which two people exchange sentiments and commitments to gain benefits not as easily available outside such a relationship. Work relationships and commitments stem from even more selfish urges.

MORAL JUDGMENT AND MOTIVATION

How realistic is this view of leadership and motivation? One way to find out is by examining your own experiences. When it comes to motivating teachers, students, and parents, for example, do you believe that what gets rewarded gets done? Or, is it your view that when individual self-interest and broader interests are in conflict people are capable of sacrificing the former for the latter? Do you believe that we are capable of responding to duties and obligations that stand above self-interest? Are we, in other words, morally responsive? These questions raise still other questions. When we choose what to do and decide what to be committed to, is the individual the primary decision-making unit and thus free to make independent decisions or do you assume, as does Amitai Etzioni (1988), that groups (ethnic and racial groups, peer groups at work, and neighborhood groups) are the prime decision-making units? In his book *The Moral Dimension,* Etzioni acknowledges that individual decision making exists but that it typically reflects collective attributes and processes, having been made within the context created by one's group memberships.

> . . . values and beliefs often—for most people typically—take precedence over self-interest.

From Etzioni's research and my extensive conversations with teachers and administrators I conclude that our connections are so important and the process of socialization that takes place as a result of our group memberships is so complete that the notion of individual decision maker is more myth than reality. Further, we humans regularly pass moral judgments over our urges, routinely sacrificing self-interest and pleasure for other reasons. Indeed, a Gallup poll (1988) revealed that 91 percent of the respondents agreed with the statement "Duty comes before pleasure," only 3 percent disagreed. Our actions and decisions are influenced by what we value and believe as well as by self-interest, and when the two are in conflict values and beliefs often—and for most people typically—take precedence over self-interest. There is, in other words, a bit of the hungry artist in all of us.

WHAT IS IMPORTANT TO TEACHERS?

What does the evidence suggest is important to teachers at work? What motivates them? What inspires them? What keeps them going even when the going gets tough? Is there a fit between the leadership practices of traditional management theory and what is really important to teachers? University of Chicago sociologist, Dan Lortie (1975), in his landmark study of teachers in Dade County, Florida, asked his respondents what attracted him to teaching. The themes that dominated their responses were serving others; the importance of working with people, particularly students; the enjoyment they receive from the job itself; material benefits; and the school calendar.

More recently, Harvard University professor Susan Moore Johnson (1990) asked similar questions to her interview study of 115 Massachusetts public, private, and parochial school teachers. Here are examples of the responses from four of the teachers she studied:

- "The way you could just look into a kid's eyes, the sparkle when you showed them something that they didn't know or that they couldn't understand. , , , There was an energy there that was quite gratifying. It made me want to keep coming back." [p. 34]
- "There was something that always attracted me to teaching. I just feel like this is my profession. My bottom line is that I love kids. I get energy from them. I just think they're the brightest people on earth." [p. 34]
- "No special reason. I was interested in language. I guest that would be the reason. I started off in Spanish. I thought that teaching would be the best way to make use of what I was studying, because I enjoyed it." [p. 36]
- "I feel that God has given all of us a gift to do something. Everybody has a strength. I really believe this strongly, that I can give children education, make them feel good about themselves, let them learn to like to read, let them look at school as Wow! This is wonderful." [p. 37]

The dominant themes that emerged from Johnson's research were working with students; an interest in the intellectual processes, puzzles, problems; the challenge of pedagogy as an occupation; a commitment to learning more or being more fully engaged in a particular subject matter area or discipline; social purposes in the one of making a difference in society; religious purposes in the sense of being called to the "ministry" of teaching; and a convenient calendar that allowed one to combine career with family or career with other life interests mostly related to personal development. The teachers reported few rewards beyond those gained by working students and from other aspects of the work itself. They were, for example, dissatisfied with low pay, lack of respect, few opportunities for advancement, lack of administrative support, unnecessary, bureaucratic demands, poorly maintained buildings, non-teaching duties, lack of parent involvement, limited autonomy, isolate from other teachers, and the lack of voice in governance and decision making. It appears from Johnson's research that the calling, sense of mission, and commitment to professional, social, or religious ideals are important enough to carry teachers despite the difficulties they encounter in the workplace. Clearly, these teachers are motivated not only by individual self-interest but also by a sense of what is morally good.

> **It appears to me that the evidence overwhelmingly suggests that self-interest is not powerful enough to account fully for human motivation.**

It appears to me that the evidence overwhelmingly suggests that self-interest is not powerful enough to account fully for human motivation. We are driven as well by what we believe is right and good, how we feel about things, and by the norms that emerge from our connections with other people. We are driven, to use Etzioni's terms, by morality, emotion, and social bonds. Together the three comprise assumptions underlying a morally based leadership: human beings pass moral judgments over their urges and as a result often sacrifice self-interest for other causes and reasons; people choose largely on the basis of preferences and emotions; and, people are members of social groups and this membership singularly shapes their individual decisions.

SOURCES OF AUTHORITY

Expanding our understanding of motivates and inspires raises the question of what should be the legitimate bases of authority for the practice of leadership. Bureaucratic, personal, and technical-rational authority pretty much dominate present thinking, and each forces us to think about leadership as something strong, direct, and interpersonal.

Bureaucratic authority relies on hierarchy, rules and regulations, mandates, and clearly communicated role expectations as a way to provide teachers with a script to follow. Teachers, in turn, are expected to comply with this script or face consequences. When this source of authority is prime the following assumptions are presumed.

- Teachers are subordinates in a hierarchically arranged system.
- Supervisors are trustworthy but you cannot trust subordinates very much.
- The goals and interests of teachers and those of supervisors are not the same and thus supervisors must be watchful.
- Hierarchy equals expertise; thus it is presumed that supervisors know more about everything than do teachers.
- External accountability works best.

Most readers will have little difficulty accepting the assertion that bureaucratic leadership is not a good idea. The underlying assumptions are too suspect. Few, for example, believe that teachers as a group are not trustworthy and do not have the same goals and interests as do their supervisors. Even fewer would accept the idea that hierarchy equals expertise. Less contested, perhaps, would be the assumptions that teachers are subordinates in a hierarchically arranged system and that external monitoring works best. Leadership theory today, for example, still relies heavily on "expect and inspect," predetermined standards, providing in-service programs for teachers and providing direct supervision. Because these practices endure, leaders must spend a good deal of time trying to figure out how to motivate teachers and what change strategies to use to get them to do things differently. Leadership, as a result, becomes a direct, intense, and often exhausting activity.

Personal authority is based on the leader's expertise in providing leadership in human relations, in using motivational techniques, and in artfully practicing other interpersonal skills. It is presumed that as a result of this leadership, teachers will want to comply with the leader's wishes. When this source of authority is prime, the following assumptions are thought be true:

- The goals and interests of teachers and supervisors are not the same.

- Teachers have needs and if these needs are met at work, the work gets done as required in exchange.
- Leaders must be expert at reading the needs of teachers and in people-handling skills in order to successfully barter for compliance and for performance increases.
- Congenial relationships and harmonious interpersonal climates make teachers content, easier to work with, and more apt to cooperate.

These assumptions lead to a leadership practice that relies heavily on "expect and reward" and on "what gets rewarded gets done." Emphasis is also given to developing a school climate characterized by a high degree of congeniality among teachers and between teacher and supervisors. The typical reaction of teachers to leadership based on personal authority is to respond as required when rewards are available but not otherwise. Teachers become involved in their work for calculated reasons, and their performance becomes increasingly narrowed.

Suggesting that practicing leadership that relies on psychological principles and personal skills may have negative consequences is likely to raise a few eyebrows. Many school leaders, for example, have worked hard to develop skill in how to motivate teachers, how to apply the correct leadership style, how to boost morale, and how to engineer the right interpersonal climate. These insights are in many ways the "core technology" of leadership. But personal authority cannot tap the full range and depth of human capacity and will and cannot elicit the kind of motivated and spirited response from teachers that will allow schools to work well. Further, overuse of personal authority raises morale as well as practical questions.

What, for example, should be the reasons why teachers should follow their principals? Is it because principals know how to manipulate effectively? Is it because principals can meet the needs of teachers and provide them with other psychological payoffs? Is it because principals are charming and fun to be with? Or is it because principals have something to say that makes sense: have thoughts that point teachers in a direction that captures their imagination; and stand on a set of ideas, values, and conceptions that they believe are good for teaches, for students, and for the school? Emphasizing the former set of questions over the latter provides for a vacuous leadership practice that can lead to what Abraham Zaleznik (1989) refers to as the "managerial mystique," the substitution of process for substance.

Technical-rational authority relies heavily on evidence that is defined by logic and scientific research. Teachers are expected to comply with prescriptions based on this source of authority in light of what is considered to be truth. When technical rationality becomes the prime source of authority the following assumptions are presumed.

- Supervision and teaching are applied sciences.
- Scientific knowledge is privileged and thus superordinate to practice.
- Teachers are skilled technicians.
- Values, preferences, and beliefs do not count very much but facts and objective evidence do.

If proposing that a psychologically based leadership practice is now dysfunctionally being overplayed in schools raises concerns, then suggesting that prime use of technical-rational authority is dysfunctional is also likely to raise concerns. We live, after all, in a technical-rational society where what is considered scientific is prized. But teaching and learning are too complex to be captured so simply. In the real world of teaching none of the assumptions for this view holds up very well, and the related practices portray an unrealistic view of teaching and supervision. There is, for example, a growing consensus that the context for teaching practice is too idiosyncratic, nonlinear, and loosely connected for simplistic conceptions of teaching to work well. As suggested earlier, teachers, like other professionals, cannot be effective by following scripts. Instead they need to create knowledge in use as they practice, becoming skilled surfers who ride the wave of the pattern of teaching as it unfolds. This ability requires a higher level of reflection, understanding, and skill than that offered under the guise of technical rationality. Further, the position of professionals need sot be superordinate to the knowledge base that supports their practice.

Two additional sources of authority for leadership practice, suggested by an expanded value structure for management theory and by acknowledging the importance of morality, emotions, and social bonds in motivation, are professional moral. The assumptions underlying the use of professional authority are:

- Situations of practice of idosyncratic and no one best way to practice exists.
- "Scientific knowledge" and "professional knowledge" are different with professional knowledge created in use as teachers practice.

- The purpose of "scientific knowledge" is to inform, not to prescribe, the practice of teachers and supervisors.
- Professional authority is not external but comes from the context itself and from within the teacher.
- Authority from context comes from the teacher's training and experience.
- Authority from within comes from the teacher's socialization and commitment to the professional ideal.

Leadership based on professional authority seeks to promote a dialogue among teachers that makes explicit professional values and accepted tenets of practice. These are then translated into standards for professional practice. With standards acknowledged, teachers are then provided with as much discretion as they want and need to hold each other accountable in meeting these standards.

One standard that needs to be developed as we move toward a practice based on professional authority is commitment to the professional ideal. The works of Albert Flores (1988), Alastair McIntyre (1981), and Nel Noddings (1984) are helpful in developing a conception of the professional ideal suitable for teaching. Professionalism, for example, tends to draw our attention to issues of competence. But competence is not enough. Key to professional autonomy is trust, and trust cannot be earned on the basis of competence alone. Virtue is the other dimension that together with competence defines professionalism. Virtue in teaching is expressed in the form of four fundamental commitments that compose the professional ideal: to practice in an exemplary way; to practice in pursuit of valued social ends; to practice with a concern not only for one's own practice but for the practice itself; and to embody the caring ethnic in one's practice.

Commitment to exemplary practice means practicing at the edge of teaching by staying abreast of new developments, researching one's practice, trying out new approaches, and so on. In a sense it means accepting responsibility for one's own professional development. To pursue valued social ends means placing oneself in service to students and parents and to the school and its purposes. It suggests, for example, that the heart of professionalism in teaching is a commitment to the caring ethic. The caring ethic requires far more than just bringing to bear a state-of-the-art technical knowledge to one's practice. Doing only this results in students being treated as clients or cases. The caring ethic means doing everything possible to serve the learning, developmental, and social needs of students as persons.

The concern for the practice of teaching itself is key to the professional ideal. There is, for example, an important difference between being concerned with one's teaching practice and being concerned with the practice of teaching. This latter concern is directed not only to broad issues of teaching knowledge, policy, and practice but to the practical problems and issues teachers face every day in their own classrooms and schools as well. As the professional ideal becomes established in a school it will no longer be acceptable for one person to teach competently without offering help to other teachers who are having difficulty. It will not be enough to have special insights into teaching but not share them with others. It will not be enough to define success in terms of what happens behind one's classroom door when the school itself may be failing.

In Moral Leadership: Getting to the Heart of School Improvement, I proposed that professional and moral authority be moved to the center of leadership practices (Sergiovanni, 1992). When professional authority is combined with moral authority the sources of authority for leadership are expanded in important and powerful ways. Moral authority is deprived from the felt obligations and duties that teachers feel as a result of their connection to widely shared school community values, ideas, and ideals. When moral authority is in place, teachers respond to shared commitments and felt interdependence by becoming self-managing. The assumptions underlying the use of moral authority are:

- Schools are professional learning communities.
- Communities are defined by their center of shared values, beliefs, and commitments.
- In communities what is considered right and good is as important as what works and what is effective.
- People are motivated as much by emotion and beliefs as by self-interest.
- Collegiality is a form of professional virtue.

As moral authority becomes the prime source for leadership practice the possibility that schools will become transformed from organizations to communities increases. Communities are defined by their center of shared values, beliefs, and commitments. Leaders in communities direct their efforts to identifying and making explicit shared values that then become sources for informal norms that govern behavior. These norms make it possible to promote collegiality as something that is internally felt and that derives from morally driven interdependence. Leaders, as a result, can rely less on external controls and more on the ability of teachers as community members to respond to felt duties and obligations. The school community's informal norm system and the internal connection of teachers to it become substitutes for leadership as teachers become increasingly self-managed.

REINVENTING LEADERSHIP

There is a consensus that leadership is an important ingredient in improving schools. At the same time, few are satisfied with the ways in which leadership has been understood and practiced, and enormous investments are being made to search for better alternatives. In my view much of this effort involves tinkering with a form of leadership that may be beyond salvaging. Leadership itself may be the culprit. No matter how enlightened, when based on bureaucratic, personal, or technical-rational authority its form is direct, external, intense, and control-oriented. As a result, leadership fails to tap fully human potential and to help teachers become self-managing. Expanding the sources of authority for leadership to include professional and moral authority and shifting the emphasis to these two provides some promising alternatives. Since both sources of authority emphasize internal motivation and promote self-management, they can become substitutes for leadership.

REFERENCES

Bennis, Warren, and Nanus, Burt. *Leaders: The Strategies for Taking Charge.* New York: Harper & Row, 1985.

Etzioni, Amitai. *The Moral Dimension: Toward a New Economics.* New York: Free Press, 1988.

Flores, Albert. "What Kind of Person Should a Professional Be?" In *Professional Ideals,* edited by Albert Flores. Belmont, Calif.: Wadsworth, 1988.

Gallup Organization Survey, conducted from the Princeton Religion Research Center, Princeton, N.J., March 11, 1988.

Johnson, Susan Moore. *Teachers at Work: Achieving Success in Our Schools.* New York: Basic Books, 1990.

Lewis, Hunter. *A Question of Values.* New York: Harper & Row, 1990.

Lortie, Dan. *Schoolteacher: A Sociological Study.* Chicago: University of Chicago Press, 1975.

McIntyre, Alastair. *After Virtue.* Notre Dame, Ind.: University of Notre Dame Press, 1981.

Noddings, Nell. *Caring: A Feminine Approach to Ethics and Moral Education.* Berkeley: University of California Press, 1984.

Sergiovanni, Thomas J. *Moral Leadership: Getting to the Heart of School Improvement.* San Francisco: Jossey-Bass, 1992.

Zaleznik, Abraham. *The Managerial Mystique: Restoring Leadership in Business.* New York: Harper & Row, 1989.

Leadership as Stewardship

by Thomas J. Sergiovanni

THE MANY FORMS OF LEADERSHIP

Leadership takes many forms. For example, a vast literature expounds the importance of practicing command leadership and instructional leadership. Both kinds provide images of direct leadership, with the principal clearly in control—setting goals, organizing the work, outlining performance standards, assigning people to work, directing and monitoring the work, and evaluating. This kind of direct leadership is typically accompanied by a human relations style designed to motivate and keep morale up.

Command and instructional leadership have their place. Heavy doses of both may be necessary in schools where teachers are incompetent, indifferent, or just disabled by the circumstances they face. But if command and instructional leadership are practiced as dominant strategies, rather than supporting ones, they can breed dependency in teachers and cast them in roles as subordinates, with the consequences discussed in chapter of Moral Leadership Subordinates do what they are supposed to, but little else. They rely on others to manage them, rather than acting as self-managers. This is hardly a recipe for building good schools.

Command leaders and instructional leaders alike are being challenged by the view that school administrators should strive to become leaders of leaders. As leaders of leaders, they work hard to build up the capacities of teachers and others, so that direct leadership will no longer be needed. This is achieved through team building, leadership development, shared decision making, and striving to

"Leadership as Stewardship" by Thomas J. Sergiovanni is excerpted by permission from *Moral Leadership: Getting to the Heart of School Improvement* by Thomas J. Sergiovanni, San Francisco: Jossey-Bass, 1992, pp. 123–134, 138–140.

establish the value of collegiality. The leader of leaders represents a powerful conception of leadership, one that deserves more emphasis than it now receives in the literature on school administration, and more attention from policymakers who seek to reform schools. Successful leaders of leaders combine the most progressive elements of psychological authority with aspects of professional and moral authority.

SERVANT LEADERSHIP

Virtually missing from the mainstream conversation on leadership is the concept of servant leadership. Greenleaf (1977) believes that "a new moral principle is emerging which holds that the only authority deserving one's allegiance is that which is freely and knowingly granted by the led to the leader in response to, and in proportion to, the clearly evident servant stature of the leader" (p.10). He developed the concept of servant leadership after reading Hermann Hesse's *Journey to the East*. Greenleaf explains:

> In this story we see a band of men on a mythical journey . . . central figure of the story is Leo, who accompanies the party as the servant who does their menial chores, but who also sustains them with his spirit and his song. He is a person of extraordinary presence. All goes well until Leo disappears. Then the group falls into disarray and the journey is abandoned. They cannot make it without the servant Leo. The narrator, one of the party, after some years of wandering, finds Leo and is taken into the Order that had sponsored the journey. There he discovers that Leo, whom he had known first as servant, was in fact the titular head of the Order, its guiding spirit, a great and noble leader [p. 7].

For Greenleaf, the great leader is a servant first.

Servant leadership is the means by which leaders can get the necessary legitimacy to lead. Servant leadership provides legitimacy partly because one of the responsibilities of leadership is to give a sense of direction, to establish an overarching purpose. Doing so, Greenleaf explains, "gives certainty and purpose to others who may have difficulty in achieving it for themselves. But being successful in providing purpose requires the trust of others" (p. 15). For trust to be forthcoming, the led must have confidence in the leader's competence and values. Further, people's confidence is strengthened by their belief that the leader makes judgments on the basis of competence and values, rather than self-interest.

When practicing servant leadership, the leader is often tempted by personal enthusiasm and commitment to define the needs of those to be served. There is, of course, a place for this approach in schools; sometimes students, parents, and teachers are not ready or able to define their own needs. But, over the long haul, as Greenleaf maintains, it is best to let those who will be served define their own needs in their own way. Servant leadership is more easily provided if the leader understands that serving others is important but that the most important thing is to serve the values and ideas that help shape the school as a covenantal community. In this sense, all the members of a community share the burden of servant leadership.

> Servant leadership is the means by which leaders can get the necessary legitimacy to lead.

In previous chapters, it was noted that schools should not be viewed as ordinary communities but as communities of learners. Barth (1990) points out that, within such communities, it is assumed that schools have the capacity to improve themselves; that, under the right conditions, adults and students alike learn, and learning by one contributes to the learning of others; that a key leverage point in creating a learning community is improving the school's culture; and that school-improvement efforts that count, whether originating in the school or outside, seek to determine and provide the conditions that enable students and adults to promote and sustain learning for themselves. "Taking these assumptions seriously," Barth argues (pp. 45-46), "leads to fresh thinking about the culture of schools and about what people do in them. For instance, the principal need no longer be the 'headmaster' or 'instructional' leader," pretending to know all, one who consumes lists from above and transmits them to those below. The more crucial role of the principal is as head learner, engaging in the most important enterprise of the schoolhouse— experiencing, displaying, modeling, and celebrating what it is hoped and expected that teachers and pupils will do." The school as learning community provides an ideal setting for joining the practice of the "leader of leaders" to servant leadership.

Command and instructional leadership, "leader of leaders" leadership, and servant leadership can be viewed developmentally, as if each were built on the others. As the emphasis shifts from one level to the next, leadership increasingly becomes a form of virtue, and each of the preceding levels becomes less important to the operation of a successful school. For example, teachers become less dependent on administrators, are better able to manage themselves, and share the burdens of leadership more fully.

The developmental view is useful conceptually, but it may be too idealistic to account for what happens in practice. A more realistic perspective is to view the expressions of leadership as being practiced together. Initially (and because of the circumstances faced) the command and instructional features of the leadership pattern may be more prominent. In time, however (and with deliberate effort), they yield more and more to the "leaders of leaders" style and to servant leadership, with the results just described.

The idea of servant leadership may seem weak. After all, since childhood, we have been conditioned to view leadership in a much tougher, more direct light. The media portrays leaders as strong, mysterious, aloof, wise, and all-powerful. Lawrence Miller (1984) explains:

> Problems were always solved the same way. The Lone Ranger and his faithful Indian companion (read servant of a somewhat darker complexion and lesser intelligence) come riding into town. The Lone Ranger, with his mask and mysterious identity, background, and lifestyle, never becomes intimate with those whom he will help. His power is partly in his mystique. Within ten minutes the Lone Ranger has understood the problem, identified who the bad guys are, and has set out to catch them. He quickly outwits the bad guys, draws his gun, and has them behind bars. And then there was always that wonderful scene at the end. The helpless victims are standing in front of their ranch or in the town square marveling at how wonderful it is now that they have been saved, you hear hoofbeats, then the William Tell Overture, and one person turns to another and asks, "But who was that masked man?" And the other replies, "Why, that was the Lone Ranger!" We see Silver rear up and with a hearty "Hi-yo Silver," the Lone Ranger and his companion ride away.
>
> It was wonderful. Truth, justice, and the American Way protected once again.

What did we learn from this cultural hero? Among the lessons that are now acted out daily by managers are the following:

- There is always a problem down on the ranch [the school] and someone is responsible.
- Those who got themselves into the difficulty are incapable of getting themselves out of it. "I'll have to go down or send someone down to fix it."

- In order to have the mystical powers needed to solve problems, you must stay behind the mask. Don't let the ordinary folks get too close to you or your powers may be lost.
- Problems get solved within discrete periodic time units and we have every right to expect them to be solved decisively.

These myths are no laughing matter. Anyone who has lived within or close to our corporations [or schools] knows that these myths are powerful forces in daily life. Unfortunately, none of them bears much resemblance to the real world [pp. 54-55].

One way in which the servant leader serves others is by becoming an advocate on their behalf. Mary Helen Rodriguez, principal of San Antonio's De Zavala School, provides an example:

> A teacher came to Mrs. Rodriguez to discuss problems she had been having in arranging a field trip for her grade level. The teacher, in reality, had begun planning too late to get the bus and sack lunch requests conveniently through the district bureaucracy for the planned day of the trip. Mrs. Rodriguez first asked the teacher how important the field trip was for the students. After a bit of discussion, Mrs. Rodriguez and the teacher decided that a trip to the zoo was indeed important given what students were studying in class at the time. Mrs. Rodriguez then immediately set about making the necessary preparations. Although it took a bit of cajoling over the telephone, sack lunches and busses were secured, and the teacher was most appreciative. The remarkable thing about this episode is the extra effort Mrs. Rodriguez put in, even though it would have been perfectly reasonable to say, "No, I'm sorry. It's just too late." In a situation where another principal might have saved her powder and not fought the system, Mrs. Rodriguez proved to be a successful advocate for the teacher and her students [Albritton, 1991, p.8].

Such ideas as servant leadership bring with them a different kind of strength—one based on moral authority. When one places one's leadership practice in service to ideas, and to others who also seek to serve these ideas, issues of leadership role and of leadership style become far less important. It matters less who is providing the leadership, and it matters even less whether the style of leadership is directive or not, involves others or not, and so on. These are issues of process; what matter are issues of substance. What are we about? Why? Are students being served? Is the school as learning community being served? What are our obligations to this community? With these questions in mind, how can we best get the job done?

PRACTICING SERVANT LEADERSHIP

Embedded in the pages of this book are practices that, taken together, show how servant leadership works and how the burden of leadership can be shared with other members of the school community. They are summarized in the following sections.

Purposing

Vaill (1984) defines *purposing* as "that continuous stream of actions by an organization's formal leadership which has the effect of inducing clarity, consensus and commitment regarding the organization's basic purposes" (p. 91). The purpose of purposing is to build within the school a center of shared values that transforms it from a mere organization into a covenantal community.

Empowerment

Empowerment derives its full strength from being linked to purposing: everyone is free to do what makes sense, as long as people's decisions embody the values shared by the school community. When empowerment is understood in this light, the emphasis shifts away from discretion needed to function and toward one's responsibility to the community. Empowerment cannot be practiced successfully apart from enablement.

Leadership by Outrage

It is the leader's responsibility to be outraged when empowerment is abused and when purposes are ignored. Moreover, all members of the school community are obliged to show outrage when the standard falls.

Leadership by outrage, and the practice of kindling outrage in others, challenge the conventional wisdom that leaders should be poker-faced, play their cards close to the chest, avoid emotion, and otherwise hide what they believe and feel. When the source of leadership authority is moral, and when covenants of shared values become the driving force for the school's norm system, it seems natural to react with outrage to shortcomings in what we do and impediments to what we want to do.

Madeline Cartwright, principal of the Blaine School in Philadelphia, regularly practiced leadership by outrage. In one instance, she was having trouble with teachers' attendance. She learned of another principal who solved this problem by answering the phone personally, and she decided to follow suit: "I started answering the phone. I say, 'Good morning, this is the Blaine School, this is Madeline Cartwright.' They hang right up. Two, three minutes later, phone rings again. 'Good morning, this is Blaine School and still Madeline Cartwright.' Hang right up. Next time the phone rang I said: 'Good morning, this is Mrs. Cartwright. If you're going to take off today, you have to talk to me. You either talk to me or you come to school, simple as that'" (Louv, 1990, p. 64). The school is the only thing that the kids can depend on, Cartwright maintains, and for this reason it is important to make sure that the teachers will show up. She tells the teachers, "As old as I am, you haven't had any disease I haven't had, so you come to school, no matter what."

> In a redefined leadership, what first appears to be lunacy may not be, and vice versa.

Some administrators who practice the art of leadership by outrage do it by fighting off bureaucratic interference. Paperwork is often the villain. Other administrators capitulate and spend much of their time and effort handling this paperwork. As a result, little is left for dealing with other, more important matters. Jules Linden, a junior high school principal in New York City, and Linda Martinez, principal of San Juan Day School, San Juan Pueblo, New Mexico, belong in the first group.

In Linden's words, "The only thing the bureaucracy hasn't tried to solve by memo is cancer . . . My rule of thumb is, when people can't see me because of the paperwork demands, I dump [the paperwork]—and most of it is not missed" (Mustain, 1990, p. 14). Martinez has devised a unique filing system to handle the onslaught of memos, rules, directives, and the like, which she receives from above: "I decided to 'bag it.' Every Friday I would clear my desk. Everything would be tossed in a garbage bag, dated and labeled weekly." Should Martinez be contacted about something filed (and that is not often the case), the proper bag is opened and dumped on the floor, and the item is retrieved for further consideration. Linda Martinez remarks, "I had never really considered my 'filing system' of garbage bags to be associated with leadership. I've been told it borders on lunacy." In a redefined leadership, what first appears to be lunacy may not be, and vice versa.

Not all schools share the dire conditions of Blaine School, and not all are deluged with a mountain of paperwork. But every school stands for something, and this something can be the basis of practicing leadership by outrage. Many administrators and teachers believe that students do not have the right to fail—that, for example, it should not be up to students to decide whether to do assigned work. Unless this belief rests on the practice of leadership by outrage, however, it is likely to be an academic abstraction rather than a heartfelt value, a slogan rather than a solution.

How is failure to complete assigned work handled in most schools? Typically, by giving zeros—often cheerfully, and without emotion. It is almost as if we are saying to students, "Look, here is the deadline. This is what you have to do. If you don't meet the deadline, these are the consequences. It's up to you. You decide whether you want to do the assignments and pass, or not do the assignments and fail." Adopting a "no zero" policy and enforcing it to the limit is one expression of leadership by outrage. It can transform the belief that children have no right to fail from an abstraction to an operational value. When work is not done by Friday, for example, no zeros are recorded. Instead, the student is phoned Friday night, and perhaps the principal or the teacher visits the student at home after brunch on Sunday to collect the work or press the new Monday deadline. If the student complains that she or he does not have a place to do homework, homework centers are established in the school, in the neighborhood, and so on.

> Adopting a "no zero" policy and enforcing it to the limit is one expression of leadership by outrage.

Just remember Madeline Cartwright, and follow her lead. Granted, not all students will respond, but I believe that most will, and those who finally do wind up with zeros will get them with teachers' reluctance. Even if the school does not "win them all," it demonstrates that it stands for something. The stakes are elevated when the problem is transformed from something technical to something moral.

As important as leadership by outrage is, its intent is to kindle outrage in others. When it is successful, every member of the school community is encouraged to display outrage whenever the standard falls. An empowered school community, bonded together by shared commitments and values, is a prerequisite for kindling outrage in others.

POWER *OVER* AND POWER *TO*

It is true that many teachers and parents do not always respond to opportunities to be involved, to be self-managed, to accept responsibility, and to practice leadership by outrage. In most cases, however, this lack of interest is not inherent but learned. Many teachers, for example, have become jaded as a result of bad experiences with involvement. Louise E. Coleman, principal of Taft Elementary School, Joliet, Illinois, believes that trust and integrity have to be reestablished after such bad experiences. When she arrived at Taft as a new principal, the school was required to submit to the central office a three-year school-improvement plan, designed to increase student achievement:

> Teachers were disgruntled at first. They were not really interested in developing a school-improvement plan. They had been through similar exercises in shared decision making before, and that's exactly what they were—*exercises*. Taft had three principals in three years. The staff assumed that I would go as others had in the past. After writing a three-year plan based on the staff's perceptions, influencing teachers by involving them in decision making, helping them to take ownership in school improvement, [we have] made some progress. Trust and integrity have been established. Most of the staff now has confidence in me. We have implemented new programs based on students' needs. The staff now volunteers to meet, to share ideas. Minority students are now considered students. Communication is ongoing. Minority parents are more involved. Positive rewards are given for student recognition. The overall school climate has changed to reflect a positive impact on learning.

Coleman was able to build trust and integrity by gently but firmly allowing others to assume leadership roles. She did not feel too threatened to relinquish some of her power and authority. Power can be understood in two ways—as power over, and as power to. Coleman knows the difference. Power over emphasizes controlling what people do, when they do it, and how they do it. Power to views power as a source of energy for achieving shared goals and purposes. Indeed, when empowerment is successfully practiced, administrators exchange power over for power to. Power over is rule-bound, but power to is goal-bound. Only those with hierarchically authorized authority can practice power over; anyone who is committed to shared goals and purposes can practice power to.

The empowerment rule (that everyone is free to do whatever makes sense, as long as decisions embody shared values), and an understanding of power as the power to, are liberating to administrators as well as teachers. Principals, too, are free to lead, without worrying about being viewed as autocratic. Further, principals can worry less about whether they are using the right style and less about other process-based concerns; their leadership rests on the substance of their ideas and values. Contrary to the laws of human relations, which remind us always to involve people and say it is autocratic for designated leaders to propose ideas for implementation, we have here a game that resembles football: everyone gets a chance to be quarterback and is free to call the play; if it is a good call, then the team runs with it.

SERVANT LEADERSHIP AND MORAL AUTHORITY

The link between servant leadership and moral authority is a tight one. Moral authority relies heavily on persuasion. At the root of persuasion are ideas, values, substance, and content, which together define group purposes and core values. Servant leadership is practiced by serving others, but its ultimate purpose is to place oneself, and others for whom one has responsibility, in the service of ideals.

Serving others and serving ideals is not an either-or proposition. Chula Boyle, assistant principal of Lee High School, San Antonio, Texas, for example, can often be seen walking the halls of the school with a young child in arm or tow. Student mothers at Lee depend on extended family to care for their children while they are in school. When care arrangements run into problems that might otherwise bar student mothers from attending class, Boyle urges them to bring the children to school. By babysitting, Boyle is serving students but, more important, she reflects an emerging set of ideals at Lee. Lee wants to be a community, and this transformation requires that a new ethic of caring take hold. Lee High School Principal Bill Fish believes that this type of caring is reciprocal. The more the school cares about students, the more students care about matters of schooling. When asked about the practice of babysitting at Lee, he modestly responds, "from time to time kids get in a bind. We are not officially doing it [babysitting] but unofficially we do what we can." His vision is to establish a day-care center in the school for children of students and teachers.

One theme of this book is that administrators ought not to choose among psychological, bureaucratic, and moral authority; instead, the approach should be additive. To be additive, however, moral authority must be viewed as legitimate. Further, with servant leadership as the model, moral authority should become the cornerstone of one's overall leadership practice.

STEWARDSHIP

The "leader of leaders" and servant leadership styles bring stewardship responsibilities to the heart of the administrator's role. When this happens, the rights and prerogatives inherent in the administrator's position move to the periphery, and attention is focused on duties and responsibilities—to others as persons and, more important, to the school itself.

Parents, teachers, and administrators share stewardship responsibility for students.

Stewardship represents primarily an act of trust, whereby people and institutions entrust a leader with certain obligations and duties to fulfill and perform on their behalf. For example, the public entrusts the schools to the school board. The school board entrusts each school to its principal. Parents entrust their children to teachers. Stewardship also involves the leader's personal responsibility to manage her or his life and affairs with proper regard for the rights of other people and for the common welfare. Finally, stewardship involves placing oneself in service to ideas and ideals and to others who are committed to their fulfillment.

The concept of stewardship furnishes an attractive image of leadership, for it embraces all the members of the school as community and all those who are served by the community. Parents, teachers, and administrators share stewardship responsibility for students. Students join the others in stewardship responsibility for the school as learning community. Mary Giella, assistant superintendent for instruction in the Pasco County (Florida) Schools, captures the spirit of stewardship as follows: "My role is one of facilitator. I listened to those who taught the children and those who were school leaders. I helped plan what they saw was a need. I coordinated the plan until those participating could independently conduct their own plans."

The organizational theorist Louis Pondy (1978, p. 94) has noted that leadership is invariably defined as behavioral: "The 'good' leader is one who can get his subordinates to *do* something. What happens if we force ourselves away from this marriage to behavioral concepts? What kind of insights can we get if we say that the effectiveness of a leader lies in his ability to make activity meaningful for those in his role set—not to change behavior but to give others a sense of understanding what they are doing, and especially to articulate it so that they can communicate about the meaning of their behavior."

This book has attempted to answer Pondy's questions. Shifting emphasis from behavior to meaning can help us recapture leadership as a powerful force for school improvement. Giving legitimacy to the moral dimension of leadership, and understanding leadership as the acceptance and embodiment of one's stewardship responsibilities, are important steps in this direction.

REFERENCES

Albritton, M. *De Zavala Elementary School: A Committed Community.* Case study, Department of Education, Trinity University, 1991.

Barth, R. *Improving Schools from Within.* San Francisco: Jossey-Bass, 1990.

Greenleaf, R. K. *Servant Leadership.* New York: Paulist Press, 1977.

Hesse, H. *The Journey to the East.* New York: Farrar, Straus & Giroux, 1956.

Louv, R. "Hope in Hell's Classroom." *New York Times Magazine,* Nov. 25, 1990, pp. 30-33, 63-67, and 74-75.

Miller, L. M. *American Spirit: Visions of a New Corporate Culture.* New York: Morrow, 1984.

Mustain, G. "Bottom-Drawer Bureau." *Washington Monthly,* Sept. 1990, p.14.

Pondy, L. R. "Leadership Is a Language Game." In M. W. McCall, Jr., and M. M. Lombardo (eds.), *Leadership: Where Else Can We Go?* Durham, N.C.: Duke University Press, 1978.

Vaill, P. "The Purposing of High-Performance Systems." In T. J. Sergiovanni and J. E. Corbally (eds.), *Leadership and Organizational Culture.* Urbana: University of Illinois Press, 1984.

Section 2

The Developmental Stages of Leadership

T ransactional and transformational leadership are different. Transactional leadership focuses on basic and largely extrinsic motives and needs of followers. It assumes, for example, that parents, teachers, and students function as rational individuals who are only motivated by self-interest. They constantly strive to figure out how to maximize their gains and to cut their losses, often without regard for the common good. Individual needs are thought to be more important than group norms. Transformational leadership, by contrast, focuses on higher-order, intrinsic, and moral motives and needs of followers. It assumes that parents, teachers, and students function as norm-referenced individuals who strongly identify with certain groups and who are influenced by these groups. They have the capacity to pass moral judgment on their individual urges and routinely sacrifice their self-interest and pleasure to advance the common good as defined by group commitments. Norms are thought to be more important than individual needs.

These differences are important. Leaders choose motivational strategies that reflect the views of human nature that they hold, but not all strategies work equally well. Students, teachers, parents, and administrators follow for three reasons: because it is in their interests to do so; because they find challenge and interest in their work; and because they value what they are doing and feel a sense of responsibility to respond. In the first instance, the motivational rule is "what gets rewarded gets done" and the driving force is extrinsic gain. In the second instance the motivational rule is "what is rewarding gets done" and the driving force is intrinsic gain. In the third instance the motivational rule is "what is good get done" and the driving force is duty or obligation.

When the first rule is used people work harder for rewards rather than for the sake of the work itself raising an important question. What happens when rewards are not available? Although what gets rewarded gets done, the reverse is also true: what does not get rewarded does not get done. Further, for this rule to keep working, leaders must be busy continuously monitoring the exchange of rewards will be of interest and which will not. Soon followers become increasingly dependent on rewards and on their leaders to motivate them. Calculated involvement and dependency can, over the long haul, discourage people from becoming self-managing and self-motivated.

Does this rule work? Yes, especially over the short haul but over the long haul there are negative consequences that must be considered. Since the rule provides the governing framework for practicing transactional leadership we can conclude that transactional leadership works too over the short term can lead to serious negative consequences over the long term.

The second rule, "what is rewarding gets done," works better than the first in building a self-managing and self-motivating followership. Relying on intrinsic forces to compel people to respond from within, the second rule provides an important bridge to transformational leadership. But this rule too results in a kind of involvement that is calculated. When, for example, teachers rely on this rule students are likely to study diligently as long as they find their studies to be interesting, challenging, and in other ways pleasurable. This is a good strategy which should be encouraged. But still, should students not find their work pleasurable they are likely to balk and become less involved. Unfortunately, learning is not always fun any more than are teaching, child rearing, looking after family needs, helping someone, donating money, or behaving as a good citizen. These are things we do because we are supposed to, not just because of the pleasure they sometimes give us.

The third rule, "what we value, believe in, and feel obligated to do gets done," works the best. This is the only rule of the three that is able to keep people involved even when what they are doing is no longer interesting or in other ways is no longer pleasurable. Instead of being involved for calculated reasons, moral reasons dominate. Most of us respond to all three of these rules at different times and for different contexts. We are involved for calculated reasons on some occasions and for moral reasons on other occasions. How these three rules are emphasized in terms of leadership can be summarized as follows:

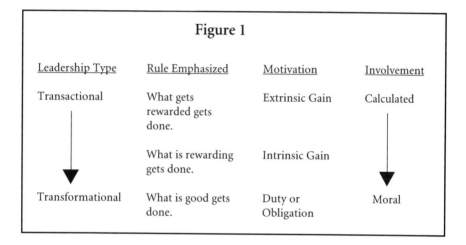

Figure 1

Leadership Type	Rule Emphasized	Motivation	Involvement
Transactional	What gets rewarded gets done.	Extrinsic Gain	Calculated
	What is rewarding gets done.	Intrinsic Gain	
Transformational	What is good gets done.	Duty or Obligation	Moral

Though at first glance the chart above seems to depict transactional and transformational leadership as two mutually exclusive options buttressed by three distinctly separate motivation rules, this is not the intent. The articles in Section 2, for example, propose that we take a developmental view of leadership. With this developmental view in mind, the first article, "Adding Value to Leadership Gets Extraordinary Results," outlines four developmental stages of leadership: leadership by bartering, leadership by building, leadership by bonding, and leadership by binding. The developmental stages acknowledge that not only are school contexts different but that people (teachers, parents, students, and administrators, as the case may be) are likely to be at different stages of readiness in how they will respond to leadership approaches. Aiming at moral involvement and being committed to a transformational approach, the leader engages others at the developmentally appropriate stage that best fits and then enables them to move through the remaining stages.

The second article, "Why Transformational Leadership Works and How to Provide It," explains the unique characteristics and conditions found in schools that seem particularly compatible with the idea of transformational leadership. Suggestions for providing this leadership are then discussed. Leadership by purpose, by empowerment, as power to accomplish, by outrage, and as moral action are explored.

The third article, "The Roots of School Leadership," compares the Pyramid, Railroad, and High Performance theories of leadership that have dominated the school scene for most of the twentieth century with an emerging moral community theory of leadership. The article argues that moral community theory fits better the unique purposes, characteristics, and work of the school. The final article in Section 2, "Why We Should Seek Substitutes for Leadership," proposes that once community images, characteristics, and norms are in place in a school they function as substitutes for leadership. Community, for example, speaks as a moral voice to teachers, parents, students, and administrators by calling them to respond to their obligations and commitments. Other substitutes for leadership discussed in this article include teacher professionalism and collegiality. Like community, they too provide norms that are difficult to ignore.

In the past we have tended to view leadership as being interpersonally based and as involved an exchange of some sort between leader and followers. This exchange is bounded by a specific incident, objective, context, and situation. Leadership takes place as such exchanges accumulate and result somehow in the achievement of specific goals. But if leadership is merely interpersonally based it will not be powerful enough to affect people for very long. And if leadership is just for the moment, we will not make the continuous and long-term process we need. Leadership needs to be viewed as an investment that contributes to the expansion of social, intellectual, and other forms of human capital. This investment quality of leadership is particularly important in schools that purport to be learning communities. Emphasizing substitutes for leadership helps us to think about leadership as an investment. The more effort a leader invests in substitutes for leadership. the more likely is she or he to be cultivating a self-managing culture in a school. Further, substitutes help build commitment to norms and ideas. And norms and ideas have a moral quality to them, calling on teachers, parents, students, and administrators to do the right thing.

Adding Value to Leadership Gets Extraordinary Results

by Thomas J. Sergiovanni

When moral authority transcends bureaucratic leadership in a school, the outcomes in terms of commitment and performance far exceed expectations.

I n 1978 James MacGregor Burns proposed a theory of leadership that has shaped new understandings of leadership practice. According to Burns, leadership is exercised when persons with certain motives and purposes mobilize resources so as to arouse and satisfy the motives of followers. He identified two broad kinds of leadership, transactional and transformative. Transactional leadership focuses on basic and largely extrinsic motives and needs; transformative, on higher-order, intrinsic, and, ultimately, moral motives and needs. This latter point is important to understanding Burns's theory. Transformative leadership is first concerned with higher-order psychological needs for esteem, autonomy, and self-actualization and, then, with moral questions of goodness, righteousness, duty, and obligation.

In his groundbreaking examination of the moral dimension in management and motivation, Amitai Etzioni (1988) provides a compelling case for moral authority as a source of motivation and a basis for management. Etzioni acknowledges the importance of extrinsic and intrinsic motivation but goes further. Ultimately, he contends, what counts most to people is what they believe, how they feel, and

"Adding Value to Leadership Gets Extraordinary Results" by Thomas J. Sergiovanni, adapted from *Educational Leadership*, May 1990, vol. 47, no. 5, pp. 23–27.

the shared norms and cultural messages that emerge from the groups and communities with which they identify. Morality, emotion, and social bonds, he maintains, are motivators far more powerful than the extrinsic concerns of transactional leadership and the intrinsic concerns of the early stages of transformative leadership.

LEADERSHIP FOR SCHOOL IMPROVEMENT

In transactional leadership, the leader and the led exchange needs and services in order to accomplish independent objectives. Leaders and followers assume they do not share a common stake in the enterprise and thus must arrive at some kind of agreement. The wants and needs of followers are traded against the wants and needs of the leader: a bargain is struck. Positive reinforcement is exchanged for good work, merit pay for increased performance, promotion for increased persistence, a feeling of belonging for cooperation, and so on. This bargaining process can be viewed metaphorically as a form of, what I have termed, leadership by bartering.[1]

Stages of Leadership

Leadership by Bartering: Leader and led strike a bargain within which leader gives to led something they want in exchange for something the leader wants.

Leadership by Building: Leader provides the climate and interpersonal support that enhances led's opportunities for fulfillment of needs for achievement, responsibility, competence, and esteem.

Leadership by Bonding: Leader and led develop a set of shared values and commitments that bond them together in a common cause.

Binding: Leader and led commit themselves to a set of shared ideas that ties them together morally as a "we" and that morally obliges them to be self-managing.

Adapted from *Value-added Leadership, How to Get Extraordinary Performance in Schools* by Thomas J. Sergiovanni, copyright © 1990 by Harcourt Brace & Company, by permission of the publisher.

In transformative leadership, by contrast, leaders and followers are united in pursuit of higher-level goals common to both. Both want to become the best. Both want to shape the school in a new direction. In Burns' (1978) words, "Such leadership occurs when one or more persons engage with others in such a way that leaders and followers raise one another to higher levels of motivation and morality" (p. 20). When transformative leadership is successful, purposes that might have started out as separate become fused. Initially, transformative leadership takes the form of leadership by building. Here the focus is on arousing human potential, satisfying higher-order needs, and raising expectations of both the leader and the led in a manner that motivates both to higher levels of commitment and performance. On one hand, leadership by bartering responds to physical, security, social, and ego needs. On the other, leadership by building responds to esteem, achievement, competence, autonomy, and self-actualization needs. The human resources leadership literature provides compelling evidence supporting the efficacy of leadership by building (see Maslow 1954, Miles 1965, McGregor 1960, Argyris 1957, and Likert 1961.)

> School improvement initiatives become real only when they become institutionalized as part of the everyday life of the school.

Burns points out that, eventually, transformative leadership becomes moral because it raises the level of human conduct and ethical aspiration of both the leader and the led. When this occurs, transformative leadership takes the form of *leadership by bonding.* Here the leader focuses on arousing awareness and consciousness that elevates school goals and purposes to the level of a shared covenant that bonds together leader and follower in a moral commitment. Leadership by bonding responds to such human needs as the desire for purpose, meaning, and significance in what one does. This stage is characterized by cultural and moral leadership.

Leadership by bartering, building, and bonding, when viewed sequentially, are developmental stages of leadership for school improvement (Sergiovanni 1990). Bartering provides the push needed to get things started; building provides the support needed to deal with uncertainty and to respond to higher levels of need fulfillment; and bonding provides the inspiration needed for performance and commitment beyond expectations.

School improvement initiatives become real only when they become institutionalized as part of the everyday life of the school. To this effort, *leadership by binding* is the fourth stage of school improvement. Binding seeks to routinize school improvements, thus conserving energy and effort for new projects and initiatives. When practicing leadership by binding, the school administrator ministers to the needs of the school and works to serve others so they are better able to perform their responsibilities. In addition to manager, minister, and servant, the leader functions as a "high priest" by protecting the values of the school (Sergiovanni 1984).

Each of the stages of leadership comprises distinct school improvement strategies. However, tactically speaking, bartering, building, bonding, and binding are leadership styles that can be used simultaneously for different purposes or with different people, within any of the stages. A recalcitrant teacher, for example, may well require leadership by bartering regardless of one's overall strategy.

> A recalcitrant teacher, for example, may well require leadership by bartering regardless of one's overall strategy.

Leadership by bartering is an especially valuable strategy when the issue is one of competence. But once competence has been achieved, one must look to the strategies of building and bonding, which will add value and help people transcend competence to reach the level of inspired commitment and extraordinary performance. Thus, depending upon whether the issue is competence or excellence leadership by bartering would make sense in one school; but, in another, leadership by building or bonding would work better. The stages of leadership and their relationship to school improvement are summarized in Figure 1. Next we look at the stages in operation in the real life experiences of a school principal.

THE STAGES IN ACTION

In 1978 Jane Kendrick arrived at Henry J. Eggers Middle School in Hammond, Indiana, as assistant principal. She found a school that was floundering.[2] Newly opened in 1973 as an open space school. Eggers was staffed by conscripted teachers, most of whom were put to work with neither understanding of how to teach in an open space setting nor commitment to the concept. Not surprisingly, Eggers had become a school with low staff morale, high dissension, student discipline problems, and below par student achievement. The personnel director later commented, "The requests for transfers out of Eggers were very high during these years. I think the percentage of requests was the highest in my tenure in personnel."

Figure 1
The Stages of Leadership and School Improvement

Leadership Type	Leadership Styles	Stages of School Improvement	Leadership Concepts	Involvement of Followers	Needs Satisfied	Effects
Value (Transactional) Leadership	Leadership as "Bartering"	*Initiation* (push) Exchanging human needs and interests that allow satisfaction of independent (leader and follower) but organizationally related objects.	Management skills. Leadership style. Contingency theory. Exchange theory. path-goal theory.	Calculated	Physical Security Social Ego	Continual performance contingent upon parties keeping the bargain struck. "A fair day's work for a fair day's pay."
Value-Added (Transformational) Leadership	Leadership as "Building"	*Uncertainty* (muddle through) Arousing human potential, satisfying higher needs, raising expectations of both leader and followers that motivates to higher levels of commitment and performance.	Empowerment. Symbolic leadership. "Charisma."	Intrinsic	Esteem Competence Autonomy Self-actualization	Performance and commitment are sustained beyond external conditions. Both are beyond expectations in quantity and quality.
	Leadership as "Bonding"	*Transformative* (breakthrough) Arousing awareness and consciousness that elevates organizational goals and purposes to the level of a shared covenant and bonds together leader and followers in a moral commitment.	Cultural leadership. Moral leadership. Covenant. Building followership.	Moral	Purpose Meaning Significance	
	Leadership as "Binding"	*Routinization* (Promoting self-management) Turning improvements into routines so that they become second nature. Ministering to the needs of the school. Being of service. Guarding the values.	Procedures. Institutional leadership. Servant leadership. Leadership by outrage. Kindling outrage in others.	Automatic	All needs are supported.	Performance remains sustained.

From: T. J. Sergiovanni (1990). *Value-Added Leadership: How to Get Extraordinary Performance in Schools.* New York: Harcourt Brace Jovanovich, pp. 39–40.

Upon arrival, Kendrick set priorities: to improve student behavior, teaching performance, and standards of professional conduct. Later (she became the principal in 1979) she fully developed the concept of learning community, organizing the school into interdisciplinary teams led by teachers who were assigned as learning community leaders. She introduced a variety of staff development programs to build the leadership capabilities of teachers and adopted the School Improvement Process (SIP) model (from the Institute for the Development of Educational Ideas) as the design for the team-based school improvement efforts.

Gradually, Eggers School developed a new identity built upon a sense of purpose and shared values. The results, as seen in achievement test scores, were nothing short of remarkable. In 1977, 8th grade average test scores on the Iowa Test of Basic Skills were as follows: vocabulary, 7.1; reading comprehension, 7.2; math computation, 6.4; math concepts, 6.4. In 1986, the average test scores, as measured by the Comprehensive Test of Basic Skills, for the same grade level were as follows: vocabulary, 8.7; reading comprehension, 8.9; spelling, 9.7; math computation, 10.0; math concepts, 9.5; social studies, 9.6.

Other recognition came to the school. Eggers was selected one of 30 Indiana middle schools successful in improving educational opportunities for its students. The Association for Supervision and Curriculum Development recognized Eggers—one of 25 middle schools across the country—for the quality of its program and its networking with other middle schools interested in school improvement. And Eggers was one of 15 Indiana middle schools awarded a $20,000 grant from the Lilly Endowment Middle Grades Schools Recognition Project. Jane Kendrick described her leadership as evolving from bartering to building and then to bonding:

> Instead of school culture and leadership behavior concerned almost exclusively with safety and security, I now participate in a culture that makes decisions about program based on the developmental and social, as well as academic needs of young adolescents . . . .For the most part, the transition . . . .was sequential, with certain skills and actions serving as steppingstones to the next level of more complicated behavior.

In 1979, when Kendrick became principal, her behavior was mainly directive: "I lectured. I told people how to think, when to think, and what to think. I made up the rules, and I enforced the rules. My actions became: tell, regulate, delegate, and evaluate." She emphasized what she wanted and then provided the right mix of rewards and punishments in exchange for desired behaviors: she exercised leadership by bartering.

Later Kendrick emphasized coaching behaviors in an attempt to upgrade her team leaders and build the teams of teachers into models of effectiveness. Adoption of the SIP model required an increased emphasis on participatory leadership development and other practices associated with leadership by building. These steps, then, provided the foundation for Kendrick to emphasize leadership by bonding. During this period, her strategies were to build common purpose, create a vision, create a leadership team, provide opportunities for teachers to become leaders, and develop collegiality as a value, which would enable leadership to be shared as teachers, parents, and students were recognized as partners. In 1987 Kendrick said, "I have observed the transformation of the norms of our faculty from those which centered around safety and discipline issues to those which center around issues of moral integrity."

As Eggers moves ahead, Kendrick believes she will become the "keeper of the vision," motivating and encouraging faculty in their efforts to do the right things for students. Further, her role will have to change from doer to servant of others who will be the doers, an emphasis associated with leadership by banking. She notes, for example, that

> Several of the faculty, and particularly members of the peer leadership team, have gone far beyond what would normally be expected in their own professional development. As they have become leaders in their own right in staff development, peer coaching, and futures planning, I must realize the inevitable—some of these individuals are going to surpass me, not only in terms of specific skill expertise, but also in terms of overall leadership ability.

The stages of leadership illustrated in the Eggers story evolved sequentially, suggesting that school improvement always begins at the bartering level. This would not be the case, however, with schools already functioning at a higher level. It is not likely, for example, that Kendrick will have to rely on leadership by bartering as her strategy when new school improvement ventures are undertaken at Eggers.

BONDING IS THE KEY

Of the four approaches, leadership by bonding is the cornerstone of an effective long-term leadership strategy for schools because it has the power to help schools transcend competence for excellence by inspiring extraordinary commitment and performance. Moreover, leadership by bonding helps people move from being subordinates to being followers.

When one understands the close links between leadership and followership, the differences between being a good subordinate and being a good follower become apparent. Good subordinates do what they are supposed to but little else. They want to know specifically what is expected of them and, with proper monitoring and supervision, will perform accordingly. They are dependent upon their leaders to provide them with goals and objectives and the proper ways and means to achieve them. They want to know what the rules of the game are, and they will play the game as required to avoid problems. For them and their leaders, life can be comfortable and easy. But for the school and the students, excellence escapes and mediocrity becomes the norm.

> Leadership by bonding is the cornerstone of an effective long-term leadership strategy for schools . . .

In contrast, good followers think for themselves, exercise self-control, and are able to accept responsibility and obligation, believe in and care about what they are doing, and are self-motivated, thus able to do what is right for the school, do it well, do it with persistence, and, most important, do it without close supervision (Kelly 1988). Followers are committed people. They are committed to something—perhaps a set of purposes, a cause, a vision of what the school is and can become, a set of beliefs about what teaching and learning should be, a set of values and standards to which they adhere, a conviction.

Subordinates are not committed to causes, values, or ideas; instead, they respond to authority in the form of rules, regulations, the expectations of their supervisors, and other management requirements. This is a crucial distinction. Subordinates respond to authority; followers respond to ideas. Since followership is linked to ideas, it is not possible to transcend subordinateness for followership in schools without practicing leadership by bonding. The concept of followership proposes a paradox: effective following is really a form of leadership (Kelly 1988). Commitment to a cause and the practice of self-management are hallmarks of good leadership and of good followership as well. The successful leader, then, is one who builds up the leadership of others and who strives to become a leader of leaders. The successful leader is also a good follower, one who is committed to ideas, values, and beliefs. When followership is established, bureaucratic authority and psychological authority are transcended by moral authority.

Then a new kind of hierarchy emerges in the school—one that places purposes, values, and commitments at the apex and teachers, principals, parents, and students below in service to these purposes. Moral authority is the means to add extra value to your leadership practice, and this added value is the secret to bringing about extraordinary commitment and performance in schools.

NOTES

1. For an elaboration of value-added leadership, the stages of leadership for school improvement and examples of practices in schools, see T. J. Sergiovanni (1990).

2. The Kendrick story is summarized from Chapter 3, "The Four Stages of Leadership for School Improvement," in T. J. Sergiovanni (1990). The full Eggers story is told in J. A. Kendrick (1987).

REFERENCES

Argyris, C. (1957). *Personality and Organization.* New York: Harper and Row.

Burns, J. M. (1978). *Leadership.* New York: Harper and Row.

Etzioni, A. (1988). *The Moral Dimension: Toward a New Theory of Economics.* New York: The Free Press.

Kelly, R. E. (Nov.-Dec. 1988). "In Praise of Followers." *Harvard Business Review.* 142-148.

Kendrick, J. A. (1987). "The Emergence of Transformational Leadership Practice in a School Improvement Effort: A Reflective Study." Doctoral diss., University of Illinois, Urbana-Champaign.

Likert, R. (1961). *New Patterns of Management.* New York: McGraw-Hill.

Maslow, A. (1954). *Motivation and Personality.* New York: Harper and Row.

McGregor, D. (1960). *The Human Side of Enterprise.* New York: McGraw-Hill.

Miles, R. (1965). "Human Relations or Human Resources." *Harvard Business Review* 43, 4: 148-163.

Sergiovanni, T. J. (1984). "Leadership and Excellence in Schooling." *Educational Leadership* 41, 5: 4-13.

Sergiovanni, T. J. (1990). *Value-Added Leadership: How to Get Extraordinary Performance in Schools.* New York: Harcourt Brace Jovanovich.

Why Transformational Leadership Works and How to Provide It

by Thomas J. Sergiovanni

> Why does transformational leadership work? What are the principles and values that characterize this leadership in action? Transformational leadership works because it fits better the way in which schools are organized and work and because of its ability to tap higher levels of human potential.

SCHOOLS ARE CULTURALLY TIGHT BUT STRUCTURALLY LOOSE

How are schools organized and how do they work? Schools are both tightly and loosely coupled places. They are, for example, tightly coupled around cultural themes and loosely coupled around management themes. This means that teachers and students are less influenced by bureaucratic rules, management protocols, leadership trades and deals, and images of rationality and are more influenced by norms, group mores, patterns of beliefs, values, the socialization process, and socially-constructed reality. There is little sustained connection between what teachers and students do and the management systems of which they are a part. At the same time there is a deep and continuing connection between what teachers and students do and the strong informal traditions and norms which exist in most schools.

"Why Transformational Leadership Works and How to Provide It" is excerpted by permission from "Advances in Leadership Theory and Practice" by Thomas J. Sergiovanni, as published in *Advances in Educational Administration,* vol.1., Greenwich, Conn.: JAI Press, 1990, pages 10–19.

Transactional leadership works best in an organizational world that is tightly structured but is loose culturally. When this is the case, management can rely on bureaucratic linkages and on leadership styles that emphasize psychological tradeoffs to get teachers to do what they are supposed to do. Cultural connections, presumed to be weak, get little attention. But when schools are characterized by loose connections structurally and tight connections culturally, it is transformative leadership that is needed. Life in schools is a struggle as administrators seek to tighten things up in a management sense while teachers respond in a cultural sense to a different set of values. For the school to work effectively a negotiated order needs to emerge from the interaction of these two dimensions.

> **When schools are characterized by loose connections structurally and tight connections culturally, it is transformative leadership that is needed.**

Leaders who rely heavily on transactional leadership are likely to view schools as being organized much like the mechanical workings of a clock. This clockworks view is appealing because we like orderly things and feel comfortable with predictability and reliability. Further, this view simplifies the task of school management. Leaders need only control and regulate the master wheel and pin and all the other wheels and pins will move responsively and in concert. This clockworks view imbues management with a sense of power and control.

Leaders who rely primarily on transformational leadership, by contrast, are likely to have a different view of how the schools they lead are organized and work. When they "open the clock" they see a mechanism going awry. The wheels and pins are not connected but instead turn and swing independently of each other (Sergiovanni, 1987). These leaders recognize that in the real world, schools operate far more loosely than is commonly assumed, certainly more loosely than organizational charts depict and often more loosely than most are willing to admit. Loose connectedness and de facto autonomy are well-documented characteristics of schools (Bidwell, 1965; Lieberman & Miller, 1984; Lortie, 1975; Morris et al., 1984; Sarason, 1971).

BUREAUCRATIC AND PROFESSIONAL IMAGES

The clockworks view of how schools work frames the way in which one thinks about teaching and teachers. Thinking in terms of tight alignment and explicit structure, one comes to see teaching as a job and the teacher as a worker. The clockworks gone awry view, on the other hand, tends to frame teaching and teachers more in the direction of a vocation engaged in by professionals. In a loosely connected world one is forced to depend less on bureaucratic rules and a highly programmed work system to get the job done and more on the commitment, ingenuity, and talent of professionals. This distinction is important because, though professionals and workers both function within the context of a work system, their relationship to this system differs.

Workers are *subordinate* to the system and are expected to follow directions and procedures as prescribed by that system. Administrators are expected to closely monitor this work system to ensure that prescriptions are followed. Professionals by contrast, are *superordinate* to their work system. Instead of the system using them, they use the system. The work of professionals emerges from an interaction between their knowledge and individual client needs. It is assumed that professionals are in command of a body of knowledge that enables them to make informed judgments in response to unique situations and individual student needs. The concept of professionalism and professional work requires a good deal of freedom. Guidelines, established principles, research findings, and best practice models are all important but they exist to inform the decisions that professionals make rather than to prescribe what it is that they do. Leadership in this context is not about prescription and trades but about informing, enabling, empowering and inspiring.

What are the values underlying transformative leadership? How do these values bring about the order and predictability schools need in a world characterized by loose coupling structurally and tight connectedness culturally? A number of values key to transformative leadership are described below (Sergiovanni, 1987).

LEADERSHIP BY PURPOSE

Transformative leaders practice leadership by purpose. Vaill (1984, p. 91) defines purposing as "that continuous stream of actions by an organization's formal leadership which has the effect of inducing clarity, consensus and commitment regarding the organization's basic purposes." Purposing is a powerful force that responds to human needs for a sense of what is important and a signal of what is of value. While many experts point out that teachers can make sense of their work lives and derive satisfaction alone, they agree that meaning, significance, and satisfaction are enhanced considerably when this process is shared (Lieberman & Miller, 1984; Lortie, 1975; Rosenholtz & Kyle, 1984). When shared meaning and significance are present, teachers respond with increased motivation and commitment. In practicing purposing, the leader's behavioral style is not as important as what the leader stands for and communicates to others. The object of purposing is the stirring of human consciousness, the enhancement of meaning, the spelling out of key cultural strands that provides both excitement and significance to one's work. (Sergiovanni & Starratt, 1983).

> **Purposing is a powerful force that responds to human needs for a sense of what is important and a signal of what is of value.**

Vision is a concept aligned with purpose that Bennis (1984, p. 66) considers to be key. To him, transformative leadership requires "the capacity to create and communicate a compelling vision of a desired state of affairs, a vision . . . that clarifies the current situation and induces commitment to the future." But purposing is more than vision. The very point of leadership is missed should leaders be remiss in expressing and articulating values and dreams. But the vision of a school must reflect, as well, the hopes and dreams, the needs and interests, the values and beliefs of the group. When a school vision embodies the sharing of ideals, a covenant is created that bonds together leader and led in a common cause. This larger concern is the point of the leadership by purpose.

LEADERSHIP BY EMPOWERMENT

Transformative leaders practice the principle of power investment. They distribute power among others in an effort to get more power in return. They know it is not power over people and events that counts but power over accomplishments and the achievement of organizational purposes. To gain control over the latter, they delegate or surrender control over the former. They understand that teachers need to be empowered to act, to be given the necessary responsibility that releases their potential and makes their actions and decisions count. Further, in a structurally loose organizational world, they are resigned to the reality that delegation and empowerment are unavoidable. But empowerment, without purposing, is not what is intended by this value. The two go hand in hand. When directed and enriched by purposing and fueled by empowerment, teachers and others respond with increased motivation and commitment to work as well as surprising ability.

> Transformative leaders know the difference between "power over" and "power to."

LEADERSHIP AS POWER TO ACCOMPLISH

Transformative leaders know the difference between "power over" and "power to." Power over emphasizes controlling people and events so that things turn out the way the leader wants. Thus, power over is concerned with dominance, control, and hierarchy as well as the striking of bargains and the making of psychological deals in the form of transactional leadership.

In reality, it is both difficult and unwise to focus on trying to program what it is that people do. To practice this kind of leadership, for example, a leader needs to be in a position of dominance, control, and hierarchy and needs to have access to the necessary carrots and sticks that provide the basis for transactional leadership. The question is, do school leaders have many carrots or sticks that teachers really care about? Are the carrots and sticks powerful enough to override the informal, often tacit cultural system to which they respond? Further, transformative leaders recognize that people do not like this form of power and will resist it both formally and informally. Moreover, even if teachers respond to this approach, it is not very effective for bringing about sustained involvement.

Transformative leaders are more concerned with the concept of power to. They are concerned with how the power of leadership can help people become more successful, to accomplish the things that they think are important, to experience a greater sense of efficacy. They are less concerned with what people are doing and more concerned with what they are accomplishing.

LEADERSHIP AND QUALITY CONTROL

To transactional leaders, quality control is a management problem that can be solved by coming up with the right controls—scheduling, prescribing, programming, monitoring, inspecting, testing and checking, and the right contingency reinforcement strategy. If leaders develop a system of schooling characterized by tight alignment, if they can monitor the system with structured and standardized supervision and evaluation, and if they can provide the right rewards then, presumably, they can ensure that things will turn out the way they are supposed to. Although transformative leaders recognize that such managerial conceptions of quality control have their place, they are likely to view the problem of quality control as being primarily cultural rather than managerial. Quality control, in their view, is more in the hearts and minds of people at work. It relates to what teachers believe, their commitment to quality, their sense of pride, how much they identify with their work, the ownership they feel for what they are doing, and the intrinsic satisfaction they derive from the work itself. Transactional leaders believe that people are driven by self-interest. Unquestionably some are. But transformative leaders believe that most people have the capacity to transcend self-interest—to care, to value, to serve, to strive for meaning and significance, to be inspired.

LEADERSHIP BY OUTRAGE

When one observes transformative leaders at work, it becomes apparent that they know the difference between sensible toughness, real toughness, and merely looking tough and acting tough. Real toughness does not come from flexing one's muscles simply because one happens to have more power than another. Real toughness is always principled. It is value-based. Transformative leaders, for example, view empowerment, delegating, sharing, and other leadership values within a target frame of reference. The eye of the target represents the core values and beliefs of the school; the distance between this eye and the outer boundary of the target represents how these values might be articulated and implemented in the practices and work of the school. Transformative leaders expect adherence to common values but provide wide discretion in implementation. They are "outraged" when they see these common values violated. The values of the common core are the nonnegotiables that comprise the cultural strands, the covenant, that defines the way of life in the school. On the other hand, teachers enjoy wide discretion in organizing their classrooms, deciding what to teach, and when and how, providing that the decisions they make embody the values that are shared and that comprise the school's covenant. In this sense, transformative leaders seek to develop schools that are both tightly and loosely structured; tight on values and loose on how values are embodied in the practice of teaching, supervision, and administration. Since, at least metaphorically, it is useful to view schools as being culturally tight and structurally loose, the job of the leader is less to establish a new culture and more to "domesticate" the existing "wild" culture by bringing it more in line with school purposes that best serve students and society.

> When administrators, teachers, and students know, agree, and believe in these defining characteristics, the concept of school culture is celebrated.

We are now at the heart of what constitutes cultural leadership. School cultures are concerned with the values, beliefs, and expectations that administrators, teachers, students, and others share. Transformative leaders help to shape this culture, work to design ways and means to transmit this culture to others, but more importantly, they behave as guardians of the values that define the culture (Sergiovanni, 1984a).

Key to the concept of purposing as a leadership value is inducing clarity, consensus, and commitment regarding the school's basic purposes. When administrators, teachers, and students know, agree, and believe in these defining characteristics, the concept of school culture is celebrated. From these defining characteristics come not only direction but the source of meaning and significance that people find important. When the leader acts as guardian of school values, the values enjoy a special verification in importance and meaning—they become real-life cultural imperatives rather than abstractions. This is the kind of leadership that not only transforms followers by arousing higher levels of need and tapping higher dimensions of human potential but that bonds followers and leaders together as part of a shared covenant.

LEADERSHIP AS MORAL ACTION

Transactional leadership view followers as means to some end held by the leaders rather than as ends in themselves. The emphasis for the leader is on understanding the psychology of followers in an effort to more effectively shape their behavior in a desired direction. If the leader is successful, then her or his goals are more likely to be achieved. In transactional leadership it is a good idea to get followers to accept the leader's goals as their own as well as to pursue them. All of this is achieved by providing the necessary inducements and incentives that respond to the followers psychology as part of an exchange.

Whether transactional leadership is moral or not depends upon whether the leader views followers as objects or things to be manipulated or as humans who are invited to engage in mutually beneficial exchanges in an aboveboard manner (Burns, 1978, p. 426). Transactional leadership does not raise moral questions if exchanges are entered into in an honest, fair, and aboveboard manner. Moral questions, however, are likely to emerge when transactional leaders rely on "salesmanship," guile, cleverness, pop psychological tricks, and other means to dupe followers into compliance. The problem with transactional leadership is not whether it is moral or not but that it tends to lead us to think of others as objects to be manipulated.

> **In transactional leadership it is a good idea to get followers to accept the leader's goals as their own as well as to pursue them.**

Even when bargains are struck in an aboveboard manner, transactional leadership seems to be characterized by a certain moral relativeness, objectivity, and rationality that relegate it to a form of technical rather than moral leadership. One of the attractions of transactional leadership is that moral relativism, objectivity, and rationality are devices that are used to avoid value conflicts and the burdens of assuming the role of moral leaders. When practicing transformative leadership, by contrast, dealing with values, covenants, and shared purposes prevents leaders from hiding in cozy places characterized by moral relativism. Moral action is unavoidable when transformative leadership is practiced. Ultimately, transformative leadership and moral leadership become one and the same. The emphasis shifts from such means values as honesty, fairness, loyalty, patience, openness, aboveboardness and so on to what Burns (1978) calls "end" values. These values are concerned with the larger purposes to be served by the actions and decisions of leaders and led and the institutions they represent. Examples are justice, community, freedom, and equality. Clearly, in transformative leadership, the emphasis is on "doing right things" rather than just "doing things right."

It is useful to distinguish between transactional leadership as leadership behavior and transformative leadership as moral action. As Starratt (Sergiovanni & Starratt, 1988) suggests, "Moral action implies some level of self initiation, of personal choosing, of a person willing to engage others for purpose beyond 'need fulfillment.' In one sense, moral action implies self fulfillment, but not in some narcissistic concentration on isolated self gratification. Rather, it is a fulfillment of the self through involvement with an authentic participation in a community's struggle to become more humane, more just, more compassionate, more loving, and yes, more productive, in the sense of making the world a healthier, safer place where the goods of the earth are shared more fairly than they are presently."

Admittedly, the culture of management in general and educational administration in particular makes it awkward to speak of transformative leadership as moral action. After all, we are not accustomed to talk about the world of leadership and organization in such sentimental language. As Starratt (Sergiovanni & Starratt, 1988) points out, "In a culture still very much dominated by a benign social Darwinism and a narrow form of individualism, to propose a morality based on the above values is an embarrassment. They are too soft, too sentimental, too unrealistic, too . . . feminine." Yet, in the final analysis, if we are to develop a theory and practice of leadership that fits the real world, we may not have much choice but to use such language. The more comfortable language of transactional leadership does not produce an efficacious leadership theory and practice able to move person and organization much beyond expected performance. Should we strive for greatness then we must accept person and organization for what they are, clusters and constellations of values. As the philosopher Broudy (1965, p. 52) reminds us:

> The educator . . . deals with nothing but values—human beings who are clusters and constellations of value potentials. Nothing human is really alien to the educational enterprise and there is, therefore, something incongruous about educational administrators evading fundamental value conflicts. A lapse in moral integrity that in a businessman or politician or a lawyer is merely deplored in an educator becomes intolerable. The public will never quite permit the educational administrator the moral latitude that it affords some of its servants. For to statesmen and soldiers men entrust their lives and fortunes, but to the schools they entrust their precarious hold on humanity itself.

At this juncture in the development of leadership theory and practice, transformative leadership offers a great deal. Building on transactional leadership, transformative appears to have the ability to tap higher depths of human potential and to produce levels of performance that are beyond expectations. It seems better fitted, as well, to an organizational world that is characterized by structural looseness and cultural tightness and seems better able to inform reflective practice. And, finally, if Green (1987, p. 108) is correct in his assertion that "The moral character of the profession does not derive from its body of technical expertise. It derives rather from the fact that a profession is a social practice that is already moral" then transformative leadership as moral agency comes closer to the point of leadership.

REFERENCES

Bennis, W. "Transformative Power and Leadership." In T. J. Sergiovanni & J. E. Corbally (eds.), *Leadership and Organizational Culture.* Urbana: University of Illinois Press, 1984.

Bidwell, C. "The School as a Formal Organization." In J. G. March (ed.), *Handbook of Organization.* Chicago: Rand McNally, 1965.

Broudy, H. S. "Conflicts in Values." In R. E. Ohm & W. G. Monohan (eds.), *Educational Administration Philosophy in Action.* Norman: College of Education, University of Oklahoma, 1965.

Burns, J. M. *Leadership.* New York: Harper & Row, 1978.

Green, T. E. "The Conscience of Leadership." In L. Shieve & M. Schoenheit (eds.) *Leadership: Examining the Elusive (1987 Yearbook).* Alexandria, Va.: Association for Supervision and Curriculum Development, 1987.

Lieberman, A., & Miller, L. *Teachers, Their World and Their Work.* Alexandria, Va.: Association for Supervision and Curriculum Development, 1984.

Lortie, D. *Schoolteacher: A Sociological Study.* Chicago: University of Chicago Press, 1975.

Morris, V. C., Crawson, R. L., Porter-Gehrie, C., & Hurwitz, E. *Principals in Action: The Reality of Managing Schools.* Columbus, Ohio: Charles E. Merrill, 1984.

Rosenholtz, S. & Kyle, S. J. "Teacher Isolation: Barrier to Professionalism." *American Educator,* 8. 1984.

Sarason, S. *The Culture of the School and the Problem of Change.* Boston: Allyn and Bacon, 1971.

Sergiovanni, T. J. "Cultural and Competing Perspectives in Administrative Theory and Practice." In T.J. Sergiovanni & J.E. Corbally (eds.), *Leadership and Organizational Culture*. Urbana: University of Illinois Press, 1984a.

Sergiovanni, T. J. "The Theoretical Basis for Cultural Leadership." In L.T. Sheive & M.B. Schoenheit (eds.), *Leadership: Examining the Elusive (1987 Yearbook)*. Alexandria, Va.: Association for Supervision and Curriculum Development, 1987.

Sergiovanni, T. J. & Starratt, R. J. *Supervision: Human Perspectives,* (3rd ed.). New York: McGraw-Hill, 1983.

Sergiovanni, T. J. & Starratt, R. J. *Supervision: Human Perspectives,* (4th ed.). New York: McGraw-Hill, 1988.

Vaill, P. B. "The Purposing of High-Performing Systems." In T. J. Sergiovanni & J. E. Corbally (eds.) *Leadership and Organizational Culture*. Urbana: University of Illinois Press, 1984.

The Roots of School Leadership

by Thomas J. Sergiovanni

> What schools need is leadership based on shared values and beliefs, rather than rules and personalities.

Defining leadership is not easy, yet most of us know it when we see it. For this reason, I find it helpful to think about leadership by thinking about leaders. Let's try it together by playing a thinking game.

Suppose one of your teachers invites you to speak to her class about leadership. You decide to ask each of the students to name one or two figures from history whom they consider to be great leaders, and to give the reasons for their choices. But sooner or later the students will want to know your own choices and reasons. So who would you pick, and what reasons would you give?

I am betting that the people you choose will share distinguishing characteristics:

- They will be people of substance.
- They will be people who stand for important ideas and values.
- They will be people who are able to share their ideas with others in a way that invites them to reflect, inquire, and better understand their own thoughts about the issues at hand.
- They will be people who use their ideas to help others come together in a shared consensus.
- They will be people who are able to make the lives of others more sensible and meaningful.

"The Roots of School Leadership" by Thomas J. Sergiovanni was originally published in the *Principal,* vol. 74, no. 2, November 1994, pp. 6–8. Reprinted by permission of NAESP (National Association of Elementary School Principals), Alexandria, Va.

Sure, many of the leaders we choose will also be good at other things. Some will be good looking, dressed for success, and have attractive personalities. Some will be highly proficient at practicing human relations and other leadership skills. And some will be management whizzes who have amazing organizational skills. But most of the great leaders-like Winston Churchill, Golda Meir, Charles de Gaulle, and Abraham Lincoln-have not had high marks for attractive personalities, interpersonal style, or management skills.

> Personality and leadership style just aren't as important as substance when it comes to leadership.

Personality and leadership style just aren't as important as substance when it comes to leadership. This observation is particularly important in the leadership of schools and other care-oriented enterprises, where purposes and relationships have deep moral overtones. Yet personality and leadership style are the characteristics most often discussed in the leadership literature, and most often sought in candidates for principalships.

When generic characteristics like leadership style and the skills of planning, organizing, controlling, and directing are separated from school contexts and substance, empty leadership is encouraged. Real leadership must be grounded in substance and idea-based.

At root, school leadership is about connecting people morally to each other and to their work. The work of leadership involves developing shared purposes, beliefs, values, and conceptions themed to teaching and learning, community building, collegiality, character development, and other school issues and concerns.

As a group, elementary and middle school principals get high marks for struggling to base their leadership on such ideas even though the system rarely supports-and sometimes punishes-such efforts. Today's theories of schooling, for example, define effective leadership as being based on rules, procedures, and other organizational factors on the one hand, and on the leader's personality and style on the other.

THREE THEORIES OF LEADERSHIP

The combination of rules-based and personality-based leadership are intrinsic in three theories that compete for attention when we think about school organization and management: the Pyramid Theory, the Railroad Theory, and the High Performance Theory.

The Pyramid Theory assumes that the way to control the work of others is to have one person assume responsibility by providing directions, supervision, and inspection. But as the number of people to be supervised increases, and as separate work sites develop, management burdens must be delegated to others and a hierarchical system emerges. Rules and regulations are developed to ensure that all of the managers think and act the same way, and these provide the protocols and guidelines used for planning, organizing, and directing.

> The Pyramid Theory . . . becomes a bureaucratic nightmare when applied in the wrong situation.

While the Pyramid Theory works well for organizations that produce standardized products in uniform ways, it becomes a bureaucratic nightmare when applied in the wrong situation. When applied to schools, for example, it simplifies and standardizes the work of principals and teachers-and the outcomes reflect this.

The Railroad Theory assumes that the way to control the work of people who have different jobs and who work in different locations is by standardizing the work processes. Instead of relying on direct supervision and hierarchical authority, a great deal of time is spent anticipating all the questions and problems that are likely to come up. Then answers and solutions are developed that represent tracks people must follow to get from one goal or outcome to another. Once the tracks are laid, all that needs to be done is to train people how to follow them, and to set up monitoring systems to be sure that they are followed.

The Railroad Theory works well in jobs that lend themselves to predictability, and where a determination of the "one best way" to do things makes sense. But when the theory is applied to schools, it creates an instructional delivery system in which specific objectives are identified and tightly aligned to an explicit curriculum and a specific method of teaching. Teachers are supervised and evaluated, and students tested, to ensure that the approved curriculum and teaching scripts are being followed. Principals and teachers use fewer skills, and student work becomes increasingly standardized.

The High Performance Theory differs from the others by de-emphasizing both top-down hierarchies and detailed scripts that tell people what to do. Decentralization is key, with workers empowered to make their own decisions about how to do things. One gets control by connecting people to outcomes rather than rules or work scripts. Borrowing from the practices of efficient business organizations, the High Performance Theory assumes that the key to effective leadership is to connect workers tightly to ends, but only loosely to means.

> The formal organization metaphor does not fit the nature of a school's purpose, the work that it does, the relationships needed for serving parents and students . . .

When the High Performance Theory is applied to schools, the ends are measurable learning outcomes. Though outcomes themselves are standardized, schools are free to decide how they are going to achieve them. Principals and teachers can organize schools and teach in ways that they think will best enable them to meet the standards. High Performance Theory emphasizes collecting data to determine how well workers are doing, and encouraging them to figure out ways to continuously improve their performance.

While the Pyramid, Railroad, and High Performance theories provide understandings that can help us make better decisions about school leadership, they also share features that make their systematic application to schools inappropriate. In all three theories, schools are perceived as formal organizations, like corporations or transportation systems. But the formal organization metaphor does not fit the nature of a school's purpose, the work that it does, the relationships needed for serving parents and students, the context of teachers' work, or the nature of effective teaching and learning environments.

Both the Pyramid and Railroad theories, for example, separate the *planning* of how work will be done from its actual *performance.* "Managers" (state or central office officials) are responsible for one, and "workers" (principals and teachers) for the other. This separation may work in running a chain of fast-food restaurants, but not for schools where professional discretion is essential to success.

In High Performance Theory, workers are provided with outcomes and other standards, and then decide how to do the work. But because planning *what* to do is separated from planning *how* to do it, problems of isolation, fragmentation, and loss of meaning remain.

When means and ends are separated, not only is professional discretion compromised, but so are democratic principles. Few parents, principals, or teachers are likely to feel empowered by being involved in decision-making processes that are limited to issues of how, but not what-of means but not ends.

THE SCHOOL AS A MORAL COMMUNITY

The alternative I propose to these leadership theories is one that views the school as a moral community. This theory has two important advantages over the school as a moral community. This theory has two important advantages over the others: It provides for moral connections among teachers, principals, parents, and students, and it helps all of them to become self-managing.

> The alternative I propose to these leadership theories is one that views the school as a moral community.

All theories of leadership emphasize connecting people to each other and to their work. These connections satisfy the needs for coordination and commitment that any enterprise must meet to be successful. The work of teachers, for example, must fit together in some sensible way for school purposes to be realized, and teachers must be motivated to do whatever is necessary in order to make this connection.

But not all theories emphasize the same kinds of connections. The Pyramid, Railroad, and High Performance theories emphasize contractual connections and assume that people are primarily motivated by self-interest. To get things done, extrinsic or intrinsic rewards are traded for compliance, and penalties for non-compliance. Leadership inevitably takes the form of bartering between the leader and the led.

Moral connections are stronger than extrinsic or intrinsic reward connections because they come from commitments to shared values and beliefs that teachers, parents, and students accept, and the obligations they feel toward each other and their work. Moral connections are grounded in cultural norms rather than in psychological needs.

With leadership firmly grounded in shared ideals, and with moral connections in place, principals, teachers, parents, and students can come together in a shared followership. The principal serves as head follower by leading the discussion about what is worth following, and by modeling, teaching, and helping others to become better followers. When this happens, the emphasis changes from direct leadership based on rules and personality, to a different kind of leadership based on stewardship and service.

Where are the roots of school leadership? San Antonio Superintendent Diana Lam answers the question this way: "I believe leadership is an attitude which informs behavior rather than a set of discrete skills or qualities . . . We need leaders who understand how children and adults learn . . . who understand how to build communities of learners."

The roots of school leadership, in other words, lie in the values, ideas, and moral authority on which it is based.

REFERENCES

Sergiovanni, Thomas J. *Moral Leadership: Getting to the Heart of School Improvement.* San Francisco: Jossey-Bass, 1992.

Sergiovanni, Thomas J. *Building Community in Schools.* San Francisco: Jossey-Bass, 1994.

Why We Should Seek Substitutes for Leadership

by Thomas J. Sergiovanni

Teachers become more committed and self-managing when schools become true communities, freeing principals from the burden of trying to control people.

I mproving schools is difficult because we give too much attention to direct leadership.[1] We focus almost exclusively on leadership as something forceful, direct, and interpersonal, instead of paying at least equal attention to providing substitutes for leadership. The more successful we are in providing these substitutes, the more likely it is that teachers and others will become self-managing. Principals will be able to spend more time on issues of substance *(What should we be doing to improve teaching and learning? How can I learn more about it?)* than process *(How can I get people to do what I think is best?)*. Further, they will not have to give nearly as much attention to formal systems of supervision and evaluation and to providing inservice training. Quality control and professional development, after all, are natural expressions of good self-management.

Whether one is willing to let go of the concepts of command and instructional and interpersonal leadership and accept the viability of substitutes for leadership depends on one's mindscape. Leadership mindscapes are shaped by what we believe and value and by our understanding of the world. They create the reality that drives our

"Why We Should Seek Substitutes for Leadership" by Thomas J. Sergiovanni is reprinted by permission from *Educational Leadership,* vol. 49, no. 5, February 1992, pp. 41–45.

CARL A. RUDISILL LIBRARY
LENOIR-RHYNE COLLEGE

leadership practice. Accordingly, I propose two questions that reveal different leadership truths depending upon how they are answered:

- Should schools be understood as formal organizations or as communities?
- What is most important when it comes to motivating and inspiring commitment and performance?

COMMUNITY OR ORGANIZATION?

Both the organization and the community metaphor ring true for certain aspects of how schools function. But it makes a world of difference which of the two provides the overarching frame. The literature in educational administration, for example, is heavily influenced by the belief that schools are formal organizations. And today's prescriptions for school leadership are based on this assumption.

> **Leadership in organizations, then, is inevitably control driven.**

Organization is an idea that is imposed from without. To ensure proper fit, schools create management systems that communicate requirements to teachers in the form of expectations. Organizations use rules and regulations, monitoring and supervising, and evaluation systems to maintain control over teachers. Leadership in organizations, then, is inevitably control driven.

In this system, principals and supervisors, by virtue of their rank, are presumed to know more than teachers and staff. Each hierarchical level is responsible for evaluating the level immediately below. Command and instructional leadership as they are now understood in schools are products of this logic.

All of this would change if community became the metaphor for schools. Communities are not defined by instrumental purposes, rationally conceived work systems, evaluation schemes designed to monitor compliance, or skillfully contrived positive interpersonal climates. Communities are defined by their centers. Centers are repositories of values, sentiments, and beliefs that provide the needed cement for uniting people in a common cause.[2] Centers govern the school values and provide norms that guide behavior and give meaning to school community life. They answer questions like, *What is this school about? What is our image of learners? How do we work together as colleagues?*

COMMUNITY NORMS

Community norms provide the school with substitutes for direct leadership. In describing her efforts to transform the Griffin Elementary School in Los Angeles into a community, for example, then-principal Yvonne Davis noted:

> We went from each teacher doing his or her own thing to teachers sharing ideas and knowing what was going on in others' rooms and throughout the different grade levels. Working together by grade levels, teachers identified pivotal concepts and skills and shared ideas on how best to teach them. Teachers felt a strong sense of accountability for students' success . . . *It was no longer a voice concerned only for "my class" or "my kids." Instead, all efforts and energies joined forces to improve the school as a whole.*[3]

As Griffin became more and more a community, the practice of teaching became less individual and more collective. As a collective practice becomes established, a principal can afford to give much less attention to the traditional management functions of planning, organizing, controlling, and leading. As Davis explains:

> My role became "acknowledger." I recognized and acclaimed good teaching, positive student results, caring parents, and progress toward our goal at every available opportunity. As people felt more appreciated, I think they worked harder and felt more confident to try out and share new ideas. At that point, my role became "supporter," "reinforcer," and "facilitator."

Teachers have a special obligation to help construct the center of shared values. This center defines certain morally held responsibilities and obligations of teachers. Among these are commitment to do one's best to make the community work and work well. This means teachers work diligently, practice in exemplary ways, keep abreast of new ideas, help other members of the learning community to be successful, and do whatever else is necessary for the community to function and flourish.

Copperopolis, California, principal Ann Leonard believes that schools should "use shared leadership with a heavy emphasis on following a vision rather than a person." Initially Leonard worried that community-building was taking precious time away from her management and supervisory responsibilities. She sees things differently now: "I've watched a metamorphosis occur. Those less-than-committed staff members who I thought needed closer supervision than I could manage are now working harder and putting in more work hours because of a shared vision we have developed together."[4]

A key question is whether the norms and core values of the community center will continue to act as substitutes for leadership even after the leader leaves.

How does she explain what is happening? "The staff is not working harder and longer because I'm a charismatic leader or because I'm using a carrot or a stick. These people are working toward realizing a goal that they believe in: their internal motivation takes much of the burden of motivation and management off me. That gives me more time to devote to finding the resources we need to realize our dreams."

A key question is whether the norms and core values of the community center will continue to act as substitutes for leadership even after the leader leaves. Newton, Massachusetts, superintendent Irwin Blumer thinks so.[5] As an administrator in the Concord and Concord-Carlisle School District, he worked to make respect for human differences and commitment to fully integrating minority students into the ongoing life of the school a core value that would guide everything that was done in the school. Reflecting on that experience he notes:

> One always wonders whether a core value has really become deeply embedded in a school system or whether it is simply something staff and others respect as long as "the leader" is there to push it . . .
> I've been away from the district now for one and one-half years and am pleased to report that the commitment of the school district is as strong and as compelling as when I was present. While it has taken different forms and different shapes under the new superintendent of schools, the commitment to the value remains.

THE PROFESSIONAL IDEAL

Both professionalism and leadership are frequently prescribed as cures for school problems, but in many ways the two concepts are antithetical. The more professionalism is emphasized, the less leadership is needed. The more leadership is emphasized, the less likely it is that professionalism will develop. Some leadership can add a measure of quality to the most professional of school settings, but leadership becomes less urgent once the wheels of professionalism begin to turn by themselves. When this happens, superintendents and principals can spend less time trying to figure out how to push and pull teachers toward goals and more time dealing with the issues of teaching and learning and ensuring financial, moral, political, and managerial support for the school.

Schools considering professionalism often turn their attention toward issues of competence: *Are teachers competent? How can we ensure that they are competent? How can we increase their competence?* Society, however, demands more than skilled service before it bestows the mantle of profession on an occupation. Professionals enjoy privileges because they can be trusted. It takes more than competence to earn trust—it takes virtue. Professionalism, therefore, is defined by competence plus virtue. Professional virtue is an idea much more at home in schools understood as communities than in schools considered formal organizations. In teaching, professional virtue is made up of four dimensions:

- a commitment to practice in an exemplary way;
- a commitment to practice toward valued social ends;
- a commitment not only to one's own practice but to the practice itself;
- a commitment to the ethic of caring.[6]

The four dimensions provide the roots for developing a powerful norm system that, when combined with the school-as-community norm system, can greatly diminish if not replace leadership as it is now practiced.

A commitment to exemplary practice means staying abreast of the latest research in practice, researching one's own practice, experimenting with new approaches, and sharing one's insights. Once established, this dimension results in a teachers accepting responsibility for their own professional growth, thus reducing the need for someone else to plan and implement staff development programs for them.

A commitment to work toward valued social ends is a commitment to place oneself in service to students and parents and to agreed-upon school values and purposes. When this ideal is in place, teaching is elevated to a form of stewardship, which in turn becomes a form of self-management.

The third dimension, a commitment to not only one's own practice but to the practice of teaching itself, forces teachers to broaden their outlook. This commitment requires that teaching be transformed from individual to collective practice. When practice is collective, the competent teacher offers help to those having difficulties. Teachers with special insights into teaching share them with others; they do not define success in terms of what happens in their own classrooms when the school itself may be failing. Teachers feel compelled to work together because of internally felt obligations.

> **To successful take hold, collegiality must be understood as a form of professional virtue.**

A commitment to the ethic of caring, the fourth dimension of professional virtue, shifts the emphasis from professional technique to a concern for the whole person. Too often, schools view students as cases to be treated rather than persons to be served. Teachers, as Noddings observes, act as models of caring when they model "meticulous preparation, lively presentation, critical thinking, appreciative listening, constructive evaluation, general curiosity."[7] An important purpose of leadership is to establish the professional ideal and community norms as conditions that make leadership no longer needed!

COLLEGIALITY

When we substitute community for organization as the metaphor for schools, we naturally turn our attention to the development of community norms and the development of the professional ideal. Somewhere along the progression toward this goal still another substitute for leadership is likely emerge—collegiality. But to successfully take hold, collegiality must be understood as a form of professional virtue.

It seems that collegiality is now understood as a synonym for congeniality or as something that results when administrators arrange for teachers to work together.[8] But neither congeniality nor contrived collegiality is powerful enough to function as a leadership substitute. Both fail the test of self-management.

Susan Moore Johnson considers teachers to be true colleagues when they are "working together, debating about goals and purposes, coordinating lessons, observing and critiquing each other's work, sharing successes and offering solace, with the triumphs of their collective efforts far exceeding the summed accomplishments of their solitary struggles."[9] Her vision for collegiality requires that it come from within. Indeed, collegiality becomes a substitute when it is driven by internal forces. Internal forces emerge when collegiality becomes an expression of professional virtue; an expression consistent with being committed to the concept of collective practice as described earlier.

There are two dimensions to collegiality as professional virtue. One is the fulfillment of obligations toward the teaching profession and toward the school as community. Both memberships provide teachers with certain rights and privileges and extract in return certain obligations and duties. Teachers have the right to expect help and support form other teachers when they need it; they are also obliged to give the same.

The second dimension involves why one behaves collegially. As Craig K. Ihara points out:

> Collegiality must then be understood as more than proper behavior toward one's colleagues. Collegiality is better defined in terms of having the proper professional attitude or orientation. To take this approach to collegiality is to consider it a kind of professional virtue . . . .[10]

Why behave collegially? Because it is effective to do so and it is good to do so. The more we come to understand collegiality in this way, the more likely it will function as a substitute for leadership.

WHAT MATTERS MOST?

The power of substitutes for leadership emerges as shared values take hold and as the idea of teachers as professionals becomes accepted. But skeptics might ask, "Are teachers able to respond to this optimistic and altruistic portrayal of leadership?"

To answer this question we need to ask another: "What motivates and inspires teachers anyway?" The rule of motivation basic to most of today's leadership practice is "what gets rewarded gets done." Though the rule works in practice, teachers wind up working for rewards rather than for the job itself. A busy kind of leadership is required to sustain the rule. Leaders must constantly monitor the exchange of rewards for rewards make most sense for different people. As a result, teachers become increasingly dependent upon leaders to motivate them. *What gets rewarded gets done discourages people from becoming self-managing and self-motivated.*

What gets rewarded gets done discourages people from becoming self-managing and self-motivated.

Imagine, for example, a school that does not specify the exact hours of work. Teachers are expected to do their work and do it well and to define their own work day accordingly. Most of the teachers rarely leave the school before 5:00 p.m.—a full two hours after the students leave. They stay because they find the work interesting and derive satisfaction from doing a good job and because they feel a sense of obligation and duty to their students—for intrinsic and moral reasons. One or two of the teachers in the school, however, consistently leave five or ten minutes after the students leave. To correct this problem the administration issues a rule requiring all teachers to stay until 3:30, rewarding those who do and punishing those who do not. After a short time the vast majority of teachers now leave at or shortly after 3:30.

What has happened in this case? Once involved for intrinsic and moral reasons, teachers are now involved for calculated reasons. Their tendency now is to calculate the payoff they receive in return for investments in their work. They are now involved for extrinsic rather than intrinsic and moral reasons.

What gets rewarded gets done assumes that people are motivated almost exclusively by self-interest. We do the things that provide the greatest gain or that incur the smallest loss. Self-interest, according to this theory of motivation, is always calculated on an individual basis. Teachers, for example, are presumed to be freestanding individuals who make decisions about gains and losses separate from others.

But self-interest is only a small part of the picture—the larger part involves our ability and desire to be morally responsive. Further, people do not calculate gains and losses alone but see their fate as connected to memberships in family, neighborhood, workplace, community, religious groups, and other groups. And when the larger interest conflicts with self, people are perfectly capable of sacrificing the latter for the former. To Etzioni,[11] for example, what matters most to people are their values, emotions, and social bonds. They are motivated in response to what they believe is right, good, and just, and to their sense of obligation. Sometimes these interests are compatible with self and sometimes not. When the two are in conflict, Etzioni argues, it is self-interest that typically loses out.

WHEN COMMUNITY TAKES HOLD

When we combine the human capacity to be morally responsive with the latest research from motivational psychologists such as Csikszentmihalyi[12] (which validates the importance of intrinsic motivation derived from the work itself) two additional motivational rules emerge:

- What is rewarding gets done.
- What we believe in, think to be good, and feel obligated to do gets done.

In both cases people get things done without direct leadership, without close supervision, and without external rewards. These additional motivational rules are difficult to put into practice in schools understood as organizations.

When schools are understood as communities, however, the two additional motivational rules come alive. Shared values, the professional ideal, and collegiality as virtue place great emphasis on the importance of rewarding work and provide the framework for sorting out commitments, duties, and obligations. In time, direct leadership will become less and less important, self-management will begin to take hold, and substitutes for leadership will become more deeply embedded in the school.

NOTES

1. This article is drawn from T. J. Sergiovanni, (1992), *Moral Leadership: Getting to the Heart of School Improvement.* (San Francisco: Jossey-Bass), particularly Chapter 4, "Substitutes for Leadership."

2. E. A. Shils, (1961), "Centre and Periphery," in *The Logic of Personal Knowledge: Essays Presented to Michael Polyani,* p. 119, (London: Routledge and Kegan Paul).

3. The Davis story is from T. J. Sergiovanni, *Moral Leadership,* op. cit.

4. Ibid.

5. Ibid.

6. The first two dimensions are from A. McIntyre, (1981), *After Virtue,* (Notre Dame, Ind.: Notre Dame University). The third is from A. Flores, (1988), "What Kind of Person Should a Professional Be?" in *Professional Ideals,* edited by A. Flores, (Belmont, Calif.: Wadsworth Publishing). The fourth is from N. Noddings, (1984), *Caring: A Feminine Approach to Ethics and Moral Education,* (Berkeley: University of California Press).

7. N. Noddings, (1986), "Fidelity in Teaching, Teacher Education, and Research for Teaching," *Harvard Educational Review* 56, 4: 503.

8. R. Barth, (1990), *Improving Schools from Within,* (San Francisco: Jossey-Bass Inc., Publishers); and A. Hargreaves, (1989), "Contrived Collegiality and the Culture of Teaching," paper presented at the Annual Meeting of the Canadian Society for the Study of Education, Quebec City, 1989.

9. S. M. Johnson, (1990), *Teachers at Work: Achieving Success in Our Schools,* p. 148, (New York: Basic Books, Inc.)

10. C. K. Ihara, (1988), "Collegiality as a Professional Virtue," in *Professional Ideals,* edited by A. Flores, p. 57, (Belmont, Calif.: Wadsworth Publishing Company).

11. A. Etzioni, (1988), *The Moral Dimension Toward a New Economics,* (New York: The Free Press).

12. M. Csikszentmihalyi, (1990), *Flow: The Psychology of Optimal Experience,* (New York: Harper and Row). See also J. R. Hackman and G. Oldman, (1976), "Motivation Through the Design of Work: A Test of a Theory," *Organizational Behavior and Human Performance* 16, 2: 250-279.

Section 3

Leading the Learning Community

These days most schools refer to themselves as learning communities but few really are. Becoming an authentic learner-centered community requires deep changes in a school's basic theory and culture. How are schools that are becoming learner-centered communities different than ordinary schools? Communities are organized around relationships and ideas. They create social structures that bond people together in a oneness and that bind them together to a set of shared values and ideas. Communities are defined by their centers of values, sentiments, and beliefs that provide the needed conditions for creating a sense of "we" and the "I" of each individual. schools that are communities reflect these characteristics by fostering tighter connections among people that create interdependencies with moral overtones. Further, they are focused on clear values and purposes that are learner-centered and rely on these values and purposes to make decisions about what to do and how to do it.

Both ordinary schools and learner-centered communities, for example, are concerned with connections. Both recognize that for schools to work well teachers, students, and parents need to be connected to themselves, to each other, to their work, and to their responsibilities. The usual way to get connections is by using rewards and punishments that trade something wanted for compliance. But in schools as learner-centered communities connections are based on commitments not trades. Teachers are expected to do a good job not so that they can get rewards from administrators, but because it is important to do so. Discipline policies are norm-based not just rule-based as in ordinary organizations. Learner-centered communities seek to connect members to what is right and wrong, to obligations and commitments, to moral agreements, and to other characteristics of norm-based social covenants. When these covenants are in place, students and teachers are compelled to action by shared commitments and values.

As a school becomes a learner-centered community it also becomes a:

- community of relationships
- community of place
- community of mind
- community of memory
- community of practice
- communication of action

In the learner-centered community *relationships* are close and informal; individual circumstances count; acceptance is unconditional; relationships are cooperative; concerns of members are unbounded and, therefore, considered legitimate as long as they reflect needs; subjectivity is okay; emotions are legitimate; sacrificing one's self-interest for the sake of other community members is common; members associate with each other because doing so is valuable as an end in itself; knowledge is valued and learned for its own sake; and students are accepted and loved because that's the way one treats community members. These kinds of relationships among people create a unity that is similar to that found in families and other close knit collections of people.

In the learner-centered community the cultivation of relationships is keyed to a sense of *place* that comes from sharing a common location. The sharing of place with others for sustained periods creates a shared identity and a shared sense of belonging that connects people in special ways.

When teachers, students, and parents are connected to the same ideas they become connected to each other as well. A community of *mind* emerges from the binding of people to common goals, shared values, and shared conceptions of being and doing. Becoming a community of relationships, place, and mind involves the development of webs of meaning that tie people together by creating a special sense of belonging and a strong common identity. Addressing the following questions helps in this development:

- What can be done to increase the sense of kinship, neighborliness, and collegiality among the faculty of the school?
- How can the faculty become more of a professional community where everyone cares about each other and helps each other to grow, to learn together, and to lead together?
- What kinds of relationships need to be cultivated with parents that will enable them to be included in this emerging community?
- How can the web of relationships that exist among teachers and between teachers and students be defined so that they embody community?
- How can teaching and learning settings be arranged so that they are more like a family?
- How can the school as a collection of families be more like a neighborhood?
- What are the shared values and commitments that enable the school to become a community of mind?
- How will these values and commitments become practical standards that can guide the lives community members want to lead, what community members learn and how, and how community members treat each other?
- What are the patterns of mutual obligations and duties that emerge in the school as community begins to be achieved?

Although not cast in stone, community understandings have enduring qualities. These understandings are taught to new members, celebrated in customs and rituals, and embodied as standards that govern life in the community. Furthermore, they are resilient enough to survive the passage of members through the community over time. As suggested by Bellah and his colleagues (1985), enduring understandings create a fourth form of community—community of *memory*. In time, communities of relationship, of place, and of mind become communities of memory that provide members with enduring images of school, learning and life. Community of memory sustains parents, teachers, and students when times are tough, connects them when they are not physically present, and provides them with a history for creating sense and meaning. The substance of a school's community of memory is often enshrined in its traditions, rites, and rituals and in other aspects of the school's symbolic life (Deal 1985; Deal and Peterson, 1991).

Perhaps the defining bench mark for identifying the learner-centered school is the presence of a community of *practice.* In traditional schools, for example, teachers are involved in their own private practices. A school with 30 teachers is defined as a collection of 30 individual practices. The principal's practice is separated from that of teachers. In the learner-centered community individual practices are not abandoned but are connected in such a way that they comprise a shared practice (Sergiovanni, 1994). There is a feeling that a single practice of teaching exists that is shared by teachers and principal alike. Teachers and principal not only identify with this practice but feel a moral obligation to help each other as connected members of the same practice. As a shared practice develops, collegiality functions at a higher level than is normally the case. The principalship too becomes a practice shared with teachers who accept responsibility for not only leadership roles but for the success of the school.

As practice becomes shared, a community of *action* begins to emerge. The familiar image of a traditional "barn raising" captures the way teachers work together when they are part of a community of action. This image stands in contrast to the "parallel play" that characterizes the work of teachers and even teams of teachers in ordinary schools. The principal's leadership is particularly important in developing and shepherding this community of action.

The first article in Section 3, "Changing our Theory of Schooling," outlines both the challenges that leaders face and the struggle that schools face as the schools strive to become a community. Using Ferdinand Tönnies' (1957) *Theory of Gemeinschaft and Gesellschaft* as a framework for understanding the differences between communities and other organizations, characteristics of communities are provided. The article concludes with a discussion of why community understandings and community characteristics are important to students and their engagement in schools and fundamental to the teaching and learning work of the school.

The second, third, and fourth articles examine relationships in community, the importance of collegiality and intrinsic motivation, and the criticalness of size as factors in helping schools become more community like.

REFERENCES

Bellah, R. N. and others. (1985). *Habits of the heart: Individualism and commitment in American life.* New York: Harper Collins.

Sergiovanni, T. J. (1994). *Building community in schools.* San Francisco, CA: Jossey-Bass.

Tönnies, F. (1957). *Gemeinschaft und Gesellschaft.* (C. P. Loomis, ed. and trans.). New York: Harper Collins (originally published in 1887).

Changing Our Theory
of Schooling

by Thomas J. Sergiovanni

C hanging our minds is always tough because of the strong connection between doing and affirmation. Current school practices have been continuously reinforced by the existing theory. As a result, their acceptance has become so automatic that they are considered to be unquestioned truths. Things are done in a certain way because they are supposed to be done that way. To change, we have to challenge practices that have always appeared sensible, and this is hard to do.

We have been taught to think of schools as formal organizations and behavior within them as organizational behavior. This forces us to think about schools in a certain way. To "organize" means to arrange things into a coherent whole. First there has to be a reason for organizing. Then all the parts to be organized are studied and mentally grouped into some kind of logical order. Next, a plan is developed that enables the elements to be arranged according to the desired scheme. Typically this is a linear process. As the plan is being followed, progress is monitored and corrections made. Finally, when the work is completed, the organizational arrangements are evaluated in terms of original intentions. These principles seem to apply whether we are thinking about organizing our bureau drawers or our schools.

Though initially organizations are creatures of people, they tend over time to become separated from people and to function independently in pursuit of their own goals and purposes. This separation has to be bridged somehow. Ties have to exist that connect people to

"Changing Our Theory of Schooling" by Thomas J. Sergiovanni is adapted from *Building Community in Schools* by Thomas J. Sergiovanni, San Francisco: Jossey-Bass Publishers, 1994, pages 1–14, by permission of the publisher.

their work and to the people they work with. In organizations the ties that connect us to others and to our work are contractual. Each person, acting separately, negotiates a settlement with others and with the organization that meets her or his needs.

Self-interest is assumed to be the prime motivation in these negotiations. Thus, for schools to get teachers to do what needs to be done, rewards must be traded for compliance. Teachers who teach the way they are supposed to get good evaluations. Good evaluations lead to better assignments and improved prospects for promotion. Bad evaluations lead to poor assignments and banishment. Teachers who cooperate get recognition, are in on the school's information system, and get picked to attend workshops and conferences. A similar pattern of rewards and punishments characterizes life within classrooms and the broader relationships that exist between students and schools.

Management and leadership are very important in schools understood as formal organizations. Since motivation comes from outside, someone has to propose and monitor the various trades that are needed. In the classroom it is the teacher and in the school it is the principal who has this job. Both are overworked as a result. Leadership inevitably takes the form of bartering. "Leader and led strike a bargain within which the leader gives to led something they want in exchange for something the leader wants" (Sergiovanni, 1990, p. 30). Students and teachers become connected to their work for calculated reasons. Students study hard as long as they get desired rewards. Teachers go the extra mile for the same reason. When rewards are reduced or no longer desired, both give less effort.

THE COMMUNITY METAPHOR

Not all groupings of individuals, however, can be characterized as formal organizations. Families, communities, friendship networks, and social clubs are examples of organized collections of people that are different. If we view schools as communities rather than organizations, the practices that make sense in schools understood as organizations just don't fit.

In communities, for example, the connection of people to purpose and the connections among people are not based on contracts but commitments. Communities are socially organized around relationships and the felt interdependencies that nurture them (Blau and

Scott, 1962). Instead of being tied together and tied to purposes by bartering arrangements, this social structure bonds people together in a oneness and binds them to an idea structure. The bonding together of people in special ways and the binding of them to shared values and ideas are the defining characteristics of schools as communities. Communities are defined by their centers of values, sentiments, and beliefs that provide the needed conditions for creating a sense of "we" from "I."

Life in organizations and life in communities are different in both quality and kind. In communities we create our social lives with others who have intentions similar to ours. In organizations relationships are constructed for us by others and become codified into a system of hierarchies, roles, and role expectations. Communities too are confronted with issues of control. But instead of relying on external control measures communities rely more on norms, purposes, values, professional socialization, collegiality, and natural interdependence. Once established, the ties of community in schools can become substitutes for formal systems of supervision, evaluation, and staff development; for management and organizational schemes that seek to coordinate what teachers do and how they work together; and for leadership itself (Sergiovanni, 1992).

> **Community members connect with each other as a result of felt interdependencies, mutual obligations, and other ties.**

The ties also redefine how certain ideas are to be understood. With community in place, for example, empowerment of teachers, students, and others focuses less on discretion and freedom per se and more on commitment, obligations, and duties that people share together. And collegiality results less from other external sources, and more from within. Community members connect with each other as a result of felt interdependencies, mutual obligations, and other ties.

A THEORY OF COMMUNITY

There is no recipe for community building—no correlates, no workshop agenda, no training package. Community cannot be borrowed or bought.

This reality makes the job of building community harder on the one hand but better on the other. Recipes are *too easy* to implement and for that reason they too often result in practices that are grafted onto the school without significantly influencing the school for very long. If we are interested in community building, then we, along with other members of the proposed community, are going to have invent our own practice of community. It is as simple, and as hard, as that. Despite the difficulties, if we are successful, our community will be not counterfeit but real.

Inventing a practice of community does not mean that we need to start from scratch. Theories of community exist that can help us. They can provide us with ideas and serve as a mental and emotional scaffold to help anchor our thoughts and transform them into a framework for community building.

> *Gemeinschaft* translates to "community" and *gesselleschaft* translates to "organization" or "society."

One "theory" that can help is known as *gemeinschaft* and *gesellschaft*. I know that the use of foreign words may seem both pretentious and distant on the surface. But *gemeinschaft* and *gesellschaft* are special words that communicate a set of concepts and ideas considered seminal in sociology. The meanings they communicate are too important to risk being watered down by less exact but more familiar synonyms. When a sociologist observes that one group of individuals, one village, or one school is more *gemeinschaft* than another, or laments the loss of *gemeinschaft* in favor of *gesellschaft,* those familiar with the terms have a comprehensive and detailed image of just what is meant. The words are metaphors that bring to mind two "ideal types," two different ways of thinking and living, two alternative visions of life.

Gemeinschaft translates to "community" and *gesellschaft* translates to "organization" or "society." The terms are attributed to the German sociologist Ferdinand Tönnies. Writing in 1887, he used the terms to describe the shifting values and orientations that occurred as we moved first from a hunting and gathering society to an agricultural society, and then on to an industrial society. Each of the societal transformations resulted in a shift away form *gemeinschaft* toward *gesellschaft;* away form a vision of life as sacred community and toward a more secular society.

Gemeinschaft

Gemeinschaft, according to Tönnies, exists in three forms: *gemeinschaft* by kinship, of place, and of mind ([1887] 1957, 42). *Gemein-*

schaft by kinship comes from the unity of being, in the sense of a "we" identity that families and extended families provide. *Gemeinschaft* of place emerges from the sharing of a common habitat or locale: this is my class, my school, my neighborhood, my town, and my country. As a result of this common membership and this sense of belonging, my being is enlarged from "I" to "we." Gemeinschaft of mind refers to the bonding together of people that results from their mutual binding to a common goal, shared set of values, and shared conception of being. Gemeinschaft of mind further strengthens the "we" identity. Though all three are helpful, gemeinschaft of mind is essential to building community within schools. As Tönnies explains, "Gemeinschaft of mind expresses the community of mental life. In conjunction with the others, this last type of gemeinschaft represents the truly human and supreme form of community" (p. 42).

> Though all three are helpful, gemeinschaft of mind is essential to building community within schools.

As we seek to build community in all three of its forms, we might ask: What can be done to increase the sense of kinship, neighborliness, and collegiality among the faculty? How can we become more of a professional community where we care about each other and help each other to be and to learn, and to lead more productive work lives? What kind of relationships need to be cultivated with parents that will enable them to be included in our emerging community? How can we help each other? How can we redefine the web of relationships that exist among us and between us and students so that they embody community? How can we arrange our teaching and learning settings so that they are more familylike? How can the school itself, as a collection of families, become more like a neighborhood? What are the shared values and commitments that enable the school to become a community of the mind? How will these values and commitments become practical standards that can guide how we lead our lives, what we learn and how, and how we treat each other? What patterns of mutual obligations and duties emerge as community is achieved?

As these questions are answered the school begins the process of transformation from an organized collection of individuals to a community of the mind. Relationships within a community of mind are based not on contracts but on understandings about what is shared and on the emerging web of obligations to embody that which is shared. Relationships within a community by kinship are based not on contracts but on understandings similar to those found within the family. Relationships within communities of place are based not on contracts but on understandings about how members will live their lives together as neighbors.

> **The connections that emerge among people from familylike feelings and relationships and from sharing a common place contribute to the development of shared values and ideas.**

Throughout this book I make frequent references to the family in illustrating how the theory of gemeinschaft can be applied to schools. Following the lead of Rev. James Close and James Wilbur (1992–1993), as they introduce "Intercessions for Holy Family Day," I use the term in its broadest sense. In their words, "The terms 'family' and 'household' have broadened in meaning beyond the usual intimate sense of spouses and children. In a conscious expression of this awareness, today's prayer of the faithful reminds us that there are also one-parent families, blended families, individuals living alone, the parish family, the community, the nation, the family of nations, and the household of faith" (p. 79).

Though not cast in stone, community understandings have enduring qualities. They are resilient enough to survive the passage of members through the community over time. They are taught to new members, celebrated in customs and rituals, and embodied as standards that govern life in the community. Enduring understandings suggests a fourth form of community—community of memory (Bellah and others, 1985). In time, communities by kinship, of place, and of mind become communities of memory.

The relationships among the four forms of community are mutually reinforcing. The connections that emerge among people from familylike feelings and relationships and from sharing a common place contribute to the development of shared values and ideas. And this community of the mind provides the basis for solidifying the feelings and identities associated with being a community of kinship and a community of place. "Whenever human beings are related through their wills in an organic manner and affirm each other we find one or another of three types of *gemeinschaft*" (Tönnies, [1887] 1957, p. 42).

Gesellschaft

Tönnies's basic argument is that as modern society advances, the world drifts further and further away from *gemeinschaft* to *gesellschaft*. Community values are replaced by contractual ones. Secondary-group relationships come to dominate primary-group relationships (Cooley, [1909] 1956). Society becomes less sacred and more secular (Becker, 1950). Life becomes more impersonal. Connections among people and between them and their institutions become contrived. Meaning and significance in life become more difficult to find. "The theory of *gesellschaft* deals with the artificial construction of an aggregate of human beings which superficially resemble the *gemeinschaft* insofar as the individuals live and dwell together peacefully. However, in the *gemeinschaft* they remain essentially united in spite of all separating factors, whereas in the *gesellschaft* they are essentially separated in spite of all the uniting factors" (Tönnies, [1887] 1957, p. 64).

The cultural ramifications of *gesellschaft* are often accompanied by psychological ones. Loneliness, isolation, and feelings of being disconnected from others and from society itself are the ones most frequently mentioned (Durkheim, [1897] 1951; Seeman, 1959). Getting ahead in a gesellschaft world is an individual endeavor; it emphasizes mastery of a set of instrumental skills that enables one to make the right transactions in an impersonal and competitive world. "In gesellschaft every person strives for that which is to his own advantage as he affirms the actions of others only insofar as and as long as they can further his interests . . . all agreements of the will stand out as so many treaties and peace pacts" (Tönnies, [1887] 1957, p.77).

Relationships in gesellschaft are contractual. This contrived exchange of sentiments, material wants and needs, sweat and toil, and even love itself reaches deep into all aspects conventional life. In Tönnies's words, "Its [gesellschaft supreme rule is politeness. It consists of an exchange of words and courtesies in which everyone seems to be present for the good of everyone else and everyone seems to consider everyone else as his equal, whereas in reality everyone is thinking of himself and trying to bring to the fore his importance and advantages in competition with the others" ([1887] 1957, p.78). Tönnies refers to these exchanges as "formless contracts."

Tönnies distinguishes between natural will and rational will in explaining the basis of relationships between and among people.

> IIn gemeinschaft, natural will is the prime motivating force. People relate to each other because doing so has its own intrinsic meaning and significance.

Social relationships, for example, don't just happen but are willed. People associate with each other for reasons. In gemeinschaft, natural will is the prime motivating force. People relate to each other because doing so has its own intrinsic meaning and significance. There is no tangible goal or benefit in mind for any of the parties to the relationship. In gesellschaft, rational will is the prime motivating force. People relate to each other to reach some goal, to gain some benefit. Without this benefit the relationship ends. In the first instance the ties among people are thick and laden with symbolic meanings. They are moral ties. In the second instance the ties among people are thin and instrumental. They are calculated ties.

The modern Western corporation is an example of *gesellschaft*. In the corporation, relationships are formal and distant, having been prescribed by roles and role expectations. Circumstances are evaluated by universal criteria as embodied in policies, rules, and protocols. Acceptance is conditional. The more a person cooperates with the organization and achieves for the organization, the more likely will she or he be accepted. Relationships are competitive. Not all concerns of members are legitimate. Legitimate concerns are bounded by roles rather than needs. Subjectivity is frowned upon. Rationality is prized. Self-interest prevails. These characteristics seem all too familiar in our schools.

The need for community becomes urgent when we consider the consequences of its loss. Students who are fortunate enough to experience belonging from family, extended family, friends, and neighbors feel attached and loved, experience the warmth and safety of intimacy, and are more cooperative and trusting of others. At an earlier time we took these values for granted. But today, in the words of Alamo Heights (Texas) superintendent Charles Slater, too often "we have lost vital parts of a good education: the neighborhood and family. While we cannot return to a simpler time, we must still find ways to give children a secure place to grow up, an opportunity to play and create and a chance to converse with adults" (1993, p. 6B).

In some respects the traditional Native American and traditional Native Canadian experiences still hang on to these values. As Brendtro, Brokenleg, and Van Bockern (1990) point out, "In traditional Native society, it was the duty of all adults to serve as teachers for younger persons. Child rearing was not just the province of biological parents but children were nurtured within a larger circle of significant others. From the earliest days of life, the child experienced a network of carting adults" (p.37). And further, kinship "was not strictly a matter of biological relationships, but rather a learned way of viewing those who share a community of residence. The ultimate test of kinship was behavior, not blood: You belonged if you acted like you belonged" and Van Bockern observe that "today's children are desperately pursuing 'artificial belongings' because this need is not being fulfilled by families, schools, and neighborhoods" (p.38).

When students experience a loss of community they have two options: to create substitutes for this loss, and to live without community, with negative psychological consequences. Unfortunately, the substitutes that young people create are often dysfunctional or distorted. Using belonging as the value, Brendtro, Brokenleg, and Van Bockern summarize some of the consequences of this loss:

Belonging

Normal	*Distorted*	*Absent*
Attached	Gang loyalty	Unattached
Loving	Craves affection	Guarded
Friendly	Craves acceptance	Rejected
Intimate	Promiscuous	Lonely
Gregarious	Clinging	Aloof
Cooperative	Cult vulnerable	Isolated
Trusting	Overly dependent	Distrustful

Some youth who feel rejected are struggling to find artificial, distorted belongings through behavior such as attention seeking or running with gangs. Others have abandoned the pursuit and are reluctant to form human attachments. In either case, their unmet needs can be addressed by corrective relationships of trust and intimacy (p. 47).

A recent report from the National Commission on Children highlights the problems America faces with loss of community. West

Virginia senator John D. Rockefeller, who chaired the commission, reported that "most American families are making heroic efforts" to maintain strong and close family ties. He noted also that "too little time, to little money, too many absent parents and overwhelming fears about children's health and safety are tearing at the seams of family life" (Cohen, 1991, p. 4). Eighty-eight percent of Americans who responded to the commission survey said it was harder to be a parent today than it used to be, 81 percent said that parents did not spend enough time with their children, 76 percent said that parents often did not know where their children were. More than half of the respondents said children are worse off today than they were ten years ago with respect to moral and religious training and parental supervision and discipline. Fully a third said that children get less love and care from parents that they did a decade ago.

> **In schools powerful and extensive norms systems develop that constitute a student subculture.**

Families fail for many reasons and often despite parents' heroic efforts. When families fail, children sometimes withdraw inward, hardening their shells and insulating themselves from the outside. But the typical response is for them to create their own "families" by turning to each other for support. Gangs, for example, provide the security, affection, and sense of belonging missing from other sources. Norms are important to young people, particularly to adolescents. In schools powerful and extensive norms systems develop that constitute a student subculture. Like any other culture these norms dictate not only how students should dress, the latest "in" language, and other harmless rituals of school life but also how students should think, what they are to value and believe, and how they should behave.

Participating in an identifiable student subculture is a healthy part of the transformation from adolescence to adulthood. But as the student subculture continues to distance itself from the mainstream norms of school and society, it strengthens its hold on what students think, believe, and do, not only about the relatively innocent rituals of adolescent life but about their studies, gang membership, sex, and alcohol and other drug abuse. A growing student subculture of this kind can come to dominate the legitimate culture of the school. When this happens, parents, teachers and principals lose control.

It is one thing to acknowledge loss of community. But proposing that schools provide substitutes for this loss can cause problems. Do we really want the school to replace the family and neighborhood? The answer of course is no. At the national level we need to commit ourselves in both rhetoric and policy to putting families and neighborhoods first. In the meantime, community building in schools can provide an important safety net as an interim strategy. Further, as schools become communities, they facilitate the strengthening of family and neighborhood.

Tönnies's use of *gemeinschaft* and *gesellschaft* as polar opposites along a continuum is an example of a strategy in sociology with a long tradition. *Gemeinschaft* and *gesellschaft* represent ideal types that do not exist in the real world in pure forms. They are, instead, mental representations that can help us categorize and explain the opposites, on the one hand, and track movement along this continuum on the other (Weber, 1949, p. 90).

Thus schools are never *gemeinschaft* or *gesellschaft*. They possess characteristics of both. Even though I argue that the balance of emphases is seriously out of kilter in most schools, it is important to recognize that the *gesellschaft* perspective is both valuable and inescapable. We live, after all, in a *gesellschaft* world—a society characterized by technical rationality. And technical rationality has brought us many gains. Without *gesellschaft* we would not have successful space program or heart transplant technology. Nor would we have great universities, profitable corporations, and workable governmental systems. There would be no hope of cleaning up the environment and we would not be able to defend ourselves. But gesellschaft brings with it its own kind of problems. As gesellschaft strengthens, gemeinschaft weakens. As gemeinschaft weakens, we experience a loss of community with all of its negative consequences.

In the extreme both *gemeinschaft* and *gesellschaft* create problems. As management expert Peter Drucker explains, "Unlike 'community,' 'society,' or 'family,' organizations are purposely designed and always specialized. Community and society are defined by the bonds that hold their members together . . . and organization is defined by its task" (1992, p. 100). He states further, "Society, community and family are all conserving institutions. They try to maintain stability and to prevent, or at least to slow, change. But the modern organization for the systematic abandonment of whatever is established, customary, familiar, and comfortable. . . . short, it must be organized for constant change" (p.96).

Too much *gemeinschaft*, in other words, blocks progress. By the same token, too much *gesellschaft* creates loss of community. The answer is not to turn the clock back to more romantic *gemeinschaft* world, but *to build gemeinschaft within gesellschaft.* We need to decide which theory should dominate which spheres of our lives. Most everyone will agree that the family, the extended family, and the neighborhood should be dominated by *gemeinschaft* values. The corporation, the research laboratory, and the court system, on the other hand, might well lean more toward gesellschaft values.

In modern times the school has been solidly ensconced in the *gesellschaft* camp (see for example Tyack and Hanson, 1982) with unhappy results. It is time that the school was moved from the *gesellschaft* side of the ledger to the *gemeinscaft* side. It is time that the metaphor for school was changed from formal organization to community.

REFERENCES

Becker, H. *Through Values to Social Interpretation.* Durham, N.C.: Duke University Press, 1950.

Bellah, R.N., and others. *Habits of the Heart: Individualism and Commitment in American Life.* New York: HarperCollins, 1985.

Blau, P. M., and Scott, W. R. *Formal Organizations.* San Francisco: Chandler, 1962.

Brendtro, L. K., Brokenleg, M., and Van Brockern, S. *Reclaiming Youth at Risk: Our Hope for the Future.* Bloomington, Ind.: National Education Service, 1990.

Close, J. J., and Wilbur, J. E. "Intercessions for Holy Family Day. "Seasonal Missalette, *Advent/Christmas,* Nov. 1992-Jan. 1993, 8 (3), 79.

Cohen, D. "Families Are Struggling Against Odds to Maintain Close Bonds, Study Finds." *Education Week,* Nov. 27, 1991, p.4.

Cooley, C. H. *Social Organization.* Glencoe, Ill.: Free Press, 1956 (Originally published 1909.)

Drucker, P. F. "The New Society of Organizations." *Harvard Business Review,* 1992, 70 (1), 95-103.

Durkheim, E. *Suicide: A Study in Sociology.* (J. A. Spalding and G. Simpson, Trans.) New York: Free Press, 1951. (Originally published 1897.)

Seeman, M. "On the Meaning of Alienation." *American Sociological Review,* 1959, 23, 783-791.

Sergiovanni, T. J. *Value-Added Leadership.* Orlando, Fla.: Harcourt Brace Jovanovich, 1990.

Sergiovanni, T. J. *Moral Leadership.* San Francisco: Jossey-Bass, 1992.

Slater, C. "Schools Called Upon to Recreate a Portion of Family Lift Lost." *The San Antonio Light,* Jan. 8, 1993, 6B.

Tönnies, F. *Gemeinschaft und Gesellschaft* (Community and Society) (C.P. Loomis, (C.P. Loomis, ed. and trans.) New York: HarperCollins, 1957. (Originally published 1887.)

Tyack, D., and Hanson, E. *Managers of Virtue: Public School Leadership in America.* New York: Basic Books, 1982.

Weber, M. *The Methodology of the Social Sciences.* (E. A. Shils and H. A. Finch, trans.) New York: Free Press, 1949.

Relationships in Communities

by Thomas J. Sergiovanni

How are relationships within communities different from those in formal organizations? The sociologist Talcott Parsons (1951, pp. 58–66) used Tönnies's concepts to describe different types of social relations. He argued that any social relationship can be described as a pattern made up of five pairs of variables that represent choices between alternative value orientations. A party to any relationship, for example, has to make decisions as to how she or he orients self to the other party. These decisions reflect the larger culture that circumscribes the relationship. As a group, the decisions represent a pattern of relationships, giving rise to Parson's term "pattern variables." The pairs of variables that compose this pattern are listed below:

affective—affective neutrality
collective orientation—self-orientation
particularism—universalism
ascription—achievement
diffuseness—specificity

In schools, principals, teachers, and students have to make decisions about how they will perform their respective roles in relationship to others. Teachers, for example, have to decide: Will relationships with students be more that of a professional expert who treats students as if they were clients (affective neutrality)? Or, will relationships be more that of a parent, with students treated as if they were family members (affective)? Will students be treated more preferentially and individually (particularism)? Will role relationships and job descriptions narrowly define specific topics for attention and discus-

"Relationships to Communities" by Thomas J. Sergiovanni is adapted by permission from *Building Community Schools* by Thomas J. Sergiovanni, San Francisco: Jossey-Bass, © 1994, pp. 21–31.

sion with students (specificity)? Or, will relationships be considered unbounded by roles and thus more inclusive and holistic (diffuse-ness)? Will students have to earn the right to

Actions toward each other are always determined by emotions (feelings of kinship, duty, or love)—or are always devoid of feelings.

be regarded as "good" and to maintain their standing in the school (achievement)? Or, will students be accepted completely, simply because they have enrolled in the school (ascription)? Do we decide that a certain dis-tance needs to be maintained in order for professional interests and concerns to remain uncompromised (self-orientation)? Or, do we view ourselves as part of a student-teacher "we" that compels us to work closely with

students in identifying common interests, concerns, and standards for decision making (collective orientation)?

Parsons believed that the five pairs of pattern variables, when view as polar opposites on a continuum, can be used to evaluate the extent to which social relations in an enterprise resemble *gemeinschaft* and *gesellschaft*. For example, though no school can be described as emphasizing affective relationships all the time or never emphasizing affective relationships, schools can be fixed on this con-tinuum based on the relative emphasis given to each of the poplar opposites. This fixing across several pairs of variables can provide us with a kind of cultural DNA (a pattern of variables, in Parson's lan-guage) that can be used to place the school on the *gemeinschaft–gesellschaft* continuum.

To illustrate the five pairs of variables (and two other pairs that are closely related) I ask you to participate in a thought exercise. In the test below, the continuum is represented in the form of a sched-ule, and the two extreme ends of the spectrum are described. Think of a school that you know well, and consider three kinds of relation-ships in the school: the way teachers relate to students, the way teach-ers relate to each other, and the way administrators relate to teachers. In each case place a mark on the line scale in the schedule that best places the relationship.

AFFECTIVE VERSUS AFFECTIVE NEUTRALITY

The parties that make up the relationship are always interested in each other—or, at the other extreme, are always disinterested.

Actions toward each other are always determined by emotions (feelings of kinship, duty, or love)—or are always devoid of feelings. In the first instance teachers always relate to students as if they were teaching their own children. In the second instance teachers always relate to students as skilled technicians who apply objective treatments to students who are clients. Principals are emotionally involved as they work with and relate to teachers—or they adopt an emotionally detached, neutral attitude.

	Affective									Affective neutrality	
Teacher-student	5	4	3	2	1	0	1	2	3	4	5
Among teachers	5	4	3	2	1	0	1	2	3	4	5
Administrator-teachers	5	4	3	2	1	0	1	2	3	4	5

COLLECTIVE ORIENTATION VERSUS SELF-ORIENTATION

The parties that make up the relationship are always motivated by common interests—or are always motivated by self-interest. In the first instance any particular action or situation is always evaluated in terms of its collective significance as defined by agreed-upon values that constitute a public moral code. In the second instance any particular action or situation is always evaluated in terms of personal significance by a private standard. At one extreme teachers, for example, always choose to help other get ready for teacher evaluations or to plan for the new year, as a reflection of their commitment to a shared sense of success. Or, at the other extreme, teachers always choose to face teacher evaluation or to plan for the new year individually and privately as they compete with each other in pursuit of more personal gains. Principals are concerned with being sure that the best decisions are made even if lines of authority have to be compromised, or they are concerned with maintaining proper lines of authority and thus insist on making decisions.

	Collective orientation									Self- orientation	
Teacher-student	5	4	3	2	1	0	1	2	3	4	5
Among teachers	5	4	3	2	1	0	1	2	3	4	5
Administrator-teachers	5	4	3	2	1	0	1	2	3	4	5

PARTICULARISM VERSUS UNIVERSALISM

The parties that make up the relationship always size up situations and make decisions on the basis of specifics that define that situation—or always on the basis of general protocols and rules. Actions are governed entirely by the particulars of the relationship itself—or actions are governed entirely by the universal norms of the system itself. In the first instance teachers always take into consideration the unique circumstances that define a discipline problem and then always create a unique resolution based on this consideration. Thus, the same discipline problem may be handled differently on different occasions. In the second instance discipline problems are always categorized by predetermined protocols and then always dealt with according to universal rules. Thus, the same discipline problem is always handled the same way whenever it appears. Teachers judge students in accordance with particular and specific standards, and the standards vary with students—or teachers judge students by universal standards, and the standards do not vary with the students.

	Particularism						Universalism				
Teacher-student	5	4	3	2	1	0	1	2	3	4	5
Among teachers	5	4	3	2	1	0	1	2	3	4	5
Administrator-teachers	5	4	3	2	1	0	1	2	3	4	5

ASCRIPTION VERSUS ACHIEVEMENT

The parties that make up the relationship always value each other for who and what they are regardless of their achievements—or always value each other for what they accomplish. Each always accepts the other as a absolute—or acceptance is always contingent on one's achievements. In the first instance students are always accepted, considered "good," and loved regardless of how well they do in school and how much they achieve. In the second instance acceptance, attributions of being a good person, and love are always contingent upon and distributed based on the extent to which students are cooperative and achieve. Teachers accept each other, help each other, and respect each other because they are members of the same school faculty—or they accept, help, and respect each other differentially, in accordance with perceptions of relative worth and relative achievement.

	Ascription										Achievement
Teacher-student	5	4	3	2	1	0	1	2	3	4	5
Among teachers	5	4	3	2	1	0	1	2	3	4	5
Administrator-teachers	5	4	3	2	1	0	1	2	3	4	5

DIFFUSENESS VERSUS SPECIFICITY

The parties that make up the relationship always view each other in less defined ways that allow for broad interaction and for concern that is widely defined— or always view each other in ways defined more narrowly by roles, role expectations, and preset work requirements. In the first instance everything about the person is always relevant on any given occasion. In the second instance relevance is always determined by role requirements of the task at hand. Principals always view teachers as whole persons to be engaged fully—or definitions and expectations. Teachers are bonded to each other as total personalities who constitute a "family"—or relate to each other in more limited ways as defined by their jobs.

	Diffuseness										Specificity
Teacher-student	5	4	3	2	1	0	1	2	3	4	5
Among teachers	5	4	3	2	1	0	1	2	3	4	5
Administrator-teachers	5	4	3	2	1	0	1	2	3	4	5

One important characteristic that differentiates *gemeinschaft* from *gesellschaft* is the relationship between means and ends. In *gesellschaft* a clear distinction is made between the two, a distinction that communicates and instrumental view of human nature and society. Within *gemeinschaft,* by contrast, the distinctions are blurred. Ends remain ends but means too are considered as ends.

On the corporate farm, for example, the land is viewed instrumentally as a means to raise crops for sale with the end being profits. Profits are important as well to the traditional family farm, but the land is not likely to be viewed quite so instrumentally. It is, instead, considered to be sacred in its own right, something to be treasured— a legacy to be passed down to subsequent generations. The land, in this case, becomes an important tie that bonds people who identify with it together into a "we" and provides them with meaning and significance. This distinction between means as ends (substantive) and means to ends (instrumental) adds a sixth pair to the schedule that can be used to evaluate your school.

In schools that resemble communities, for example, teachers care about the subjects they teach. They communicate to students that what is being taught is valuable in its own right and not a mere means to some end. Reverence for what is being taught is modeled by a spirit of inquiry and by the teacher}s commitment to being a learner. This stance pays dividends in increased student learning. Many of the other pattern variables speak to the principle: "You need to know students well to teach them well. "This one adds the principle: "You need to be passionate about what you teach if students are to value what is taught."

SUBSTANTIVE VERSUS INSTRUMENTAL

The partners that make up the relationship always view means as ends equal to ends — or always make a clear distinction between means and ends. Discipline policies and rules are always considered to be moral standards to be celebrated in their own right — or are always considered as means to manage the behavior of students. The subjects taught are viewed entirely as knowledge to be valued and enjoyed — or are always viewed as content to be mastered in order to get good grades and high test scores. In the first instance principals emphasize improving the quality of the teachers' workplace because that is a good thing to do. In the second instance principals work to improve the quality of the teachers' workplace as a way to motivate them to perform. In the first instance students are fed because loving, compassionate people feed hungry children. In the second instance the purpose of the school breakfast program is to relieve the hunger that keeps children from leaning (Noddings, 1992, p. 13). Students study only because they value knowledge as an end in itself—or only to win approval, get promoted, or perhaps to qualify for the driver's education program.

	Substantive						Instrumental				
Teacher-student	5	4	3	2	1	0	1	2	3	4	5
Among teachers	5	4	3	2	1	0	1	2	3	4	5
Administrator-teachers	5	4	3	2	1	0	1	2	3	4	5

ALTRUISM VERSUS EGOCENTRISM

Gemeinschaft and *gesellschaft* provide different ties for connecting people to each other and for connecting them to their work. In the school as community, relationships are both close and informal. Individual circumstances count. Acceptance is unconditional. Relationships are cooperative. Concerns of members are unbounded, and thus considered legitimate. Sacrificing one's self-interest for the sake of other community members is common. Member associate with each other because doing so is valuable as an end in itself. Knowledge is valued and learned for its own sake, not just as a means to get something or get somewhere. Children are accepted and loved because that's the way one treats community members. These community characteristics emerge in part because of the ties of kinship and in part because of the sense of identity that is created by sharing a common place such as a classroom or a school. But the ties that bond and bind the most are those that emerge from a compact of mutual shared obligations and commitments, a common purpose. These are the ingredients needed to create a community of the mind.

> In schools that resemble communities . . . teachers communicate to students that what is being taught is valuable in its own right and not a mere means to some end.

Philosopher Mary Rousseau (1991) believes that the key to determining whether community will be authentic or counterfeit is the motives that bring people together. To her it is altruistic love that differentiates authentic from counterfeit. Words like "altruism" and "love can make us uncomfortable. Our *gesellschaft* theories of schooling, I fear, have conditioned us to adopt an impersonal, bureaucratic, professional, managerial, and technical language. Students are clients to be treated and have problems to be solved. Learning is equated with training. Teaching becomes instruction. Deciding, sharing, and reflecting together is labeled "site-based management." Concerns about what we are doing, why we are doing it become "total quality management." Students who are interested in what is being taught and are showing it are "off task." I fear that this language distances us from the real concerns of people and the real problems of schooling. If we are going to be serious this language barrier by speaking more directly and more humanly about schooling.

To be blunt about it, we cannot achieve community unless we commit ourselves to the principle "love thy neighbor as thyself." Yes, these are sacred words but then again community is a sacred idea. Loving in this sense does not mean that I want to spend my summer vacation with my neighbor or that I want to become her or his telephone companion. It certainly does not mean falling in love in the romantic sense, or having other unusual feelings off affection, warmth, tenderness, or lust. These examples are more descriptive of egocentric love than altruistic love.

> To be blunt about it, we cannot achieve community unless we commit ourselves to the principle "love thy neighbor as thyself."

Egocentric love is emotionally and physically self-gratifying. When egocentric love is the motive, each of the parties to the relationship enter into an implicit contract with the other for the exchange of needs and satisfactions that benefit both. As Mary Rousseau points out, "Contracts, inherently egocentric in their motivation, can only link people together in the same place at the same time, to share a common activity or project. But since those who love contractually are seeking their own fulfillment as their end, looking to other people as the means to their own pleasure or utility, they forge no existential bonds with each other" (p. 49).

Webster defines altruism as benevolent concern for the welfare of others, as selflessness. Love is defined as deep devotion and good will that comes from and contributes to feelings of brotherhood and sisterhood. Altruistic love is an expression of selfless concern for others that stems from devotion or obligation. At its heart, altruistic love is more cultural than psychological. It can exist even if community by blood and community of place are absent. Community of the mind is enough to sustain altruistic love.

For example, teachers and administrators who work at the central office are not physically close to teachers, administrators, and students in a particular school. Yet they can demonstrate altruistic love when motivated by devotion and duty and when they show selfless concern for the welfare of that school. When they do this, they qualify as member of that particular community.

Strictly speaking, altruistic love and egocentric love are not opposite poles of the same continuum. But arranging them in this way is still useful for our purposes. Considering altruistic and ego-centric love provides us with another set of ideas that can be used to evaluate the gemeinschaft and gesellschaft qualities of a particular school.

	Altruistic love					Egocentric love				
Teacher-student	5	4	3	2	1	0	1	2	3	4	5
Among teachers	5	4	3	2	1	0	1	2	3	4	5
Administrator-teachers	5	4	3	2	1	0	1	2	3	4	5

In sum, we can access the extent to which relationships within a school embody community by describing them using Parson's five pairs of pattern variables and two additional pairs that constitute extended pattern of seven. In Table 2.1, this extended pattern is arranged in the form of an inventory, "Profile of Community." The more gemeinschaft-like is the pattern, the more community like is the school. The more gesellschaft-like is the pattern, the more appropriate is the metaphor "formal organization."

Table 2.1
Profiles of Community

School as Community (Gemeinschaft)	Teacher's relationship with students 5 4 3 2 1 0 1 2 3 4 5	School as Formal Organization (Gesellschaft)
Affective	• • • • • • • • • • •	Affective neutrality
Collective orientation	• • • • • • • • • • •	Self-orientation
Particularism	• • • • • • • • • • •	Universalism
Ascription	• • • • • • • • • • •	Achievement
Diffuseness	• • • • • • • • • • •	Specificity
Substantive	• • • • • • • • • • •	Instrumental
Altruistic love	• • • • • • • • • • •	Ego-centered love

continued on next page

Table 2.1
Profiles of Community cont.

School as Community (Gemeinschaft)													School as Formal Organization (Gesellschaft)
			Relationships among teachers										
	5	4	3	2	1	0	1	2	3	4	5		
Affective	·	·	·	·	·	·	·	·	·	·	·		Affective neutrality
Collective orientation	·	·	·	·	·	·	·	·	·	·	·		Self-orientation
Particularism	·	·	·	·	·	·	·	·	·	·	·		Universalism
Ascription	·	·	·	·	·	·	·	·	·	·	·		Achievement
Diffuseness	·	·	·	·	·	·	·	·	·	·	·		Specificity
Substantive	·	·	·	·	·	·	·	·	·	·	·		Instrumental
Altruistic love	·	·	·	·	·	·	·	·	·	·	·		Ego-centered love
			Administrators' relationships with teachers										
	5	4	3	2	1	0	1	2	3	4	5		
Affective	·	·	·	·	·	·	·	·	·	·	·		Affective neutrality
Collective orientation	·	·	·	·	·	·	·	·	·	·	·		Self-orientation
Particularism	·	·	·	·	·	·	·	·	·	·	·		Universalism
Ascription	·	·	·	·	·	·	·	·	·	·	·		Achievement
Diffuseness	·	·	·	·	·	·	·	·	·	·	·		Specificity
Substantive	·	·	·	·	·	·	·	·	·	·	·		Instrumental
Altruistic love	·	·	·	·	·	·	·	·	·	·	·		Ego-centered love

REFERENCES

Noddings, N. *The Challenge to Care in Schools: An Alternative Approach to Education.* New York: Teachers College Press, 1992.

Parsons, T. *The Social System.* New York: Free Press, 1951.

Rousseau, M. F. *Community: The Tie That Binds.* New York: University Press of America, 1991.

Getting Practical
Enhancing Collegiality and Intrinsic Motivation

by Thomas J. Sergiovanni

ollegiality and intrinsic motivation are both powerful and practical school-improvement strategies. They are the value-added leadership dimensions that are necessary to build a professional culture of teaching with standards, norms, and practices aligned to excellence. This chapter demonstrates that building a professional culture of teaching is the only alternative available to us if we seek excellence in a world of schooling that is loosely connected managerially but tightly connected culturally. It is argued that the peculiar combination of looseness and tightness that characterizes schools means that nothing else will work. For this reason value-added leader consider collegiality and intrinsic motivation to be practical school-improvement strategies.

Despite the importance and practicality of collegiality and intrinsic motivation, the two are sometimes mistrusted and often misunderstood. Policymakers and school administrators, for example, often confuse congeniality with collegiality and extrinsic motivation with intrinsic. Let's first examine collegiality and then turn our attention to intrinsic motivation.

• Congeniality refers to the friendly human relationships that exist among teachers and is characterized by the loyalty, trust, and easy conversation that result in the development of a closely knit social group.

"Getting Practical: Enhancing Collegiality and Intrinsic Motivation" by Thomas J. Sergiovanni is from *Value-Added Leadership: How to Get Extraordinary Performance in Schools* by Thomas J. Sergiovanni, Copyright © 1990 by Harcourt, Brace and Company, reprinted with permission of the publisher.

- Collegiality refers to the existence of high levels of collaboration among teachers, and is characterized by mutual respect, shared work values, cooperation, and specific conversation about teaching and learning.
- When congeniality is high, a strong informal culture aligned with social norms emerges in the school. The norms may or may not be aligned with school purposes. Sometimes the norms contribute to and at other times interfere with increased commitment and extraordinary performance.
- When collegiality is high, a strong professional culture held together by shared work norms emerges in the school. The norms are aligned with school purposes, contributing consistently to increased commitment and extraordinary performance.

Congeniality and collegiality are very different. Congeniality refers to friendly human relationships and the development of strong supporting social norms that are independent from the standards of the teaching profession and the purposes and work of the school.

Collegiality, by contrast, refers to principals and teachers sharing, helping, learning and working together in response to strong supporting work norms that emerge from professional standards and school purposes.

Both congeniality and collegiality are desirable and together comprise value and value-added dimensions of leadership. However, congeniality without collegiality can result in the development of informal norms that may be work-restricting resulting in less effective teaching and learning for students. For example, teachers might informally agree that the price of membership in the social group is to give a "fair day's work for a fair day's pay" but not to exceed this limit. Teachers are expected to do what they are "supposed to," thus avoiding problems with management, but never more. They become oriented to the minimum, not the maximum necessary for quality schooling. New teachers who want to join the group will have to abide by the informal rules of this work-restrictive culture in exchange for accepted membership.

When congeniality is combined with collegiality, work-enhancing values and norms are actually reinforced; but this ideal combination is not necessary for excellence. Many cases exist in both the corporate world and schools where the climate is "strictly businesslike." Shared work norms are strong and people cooperate. They are cordial to each other but are not particularly close socially. Though value-added leaders may enjoy and promote congeniality, their emphasis is on providing the climate and conditions that enhance the norms of collegiality.

Recent research independently reported by University of California, Berkeley professor, Judith Warren Little, and Susan Rosenholtz of the University of Illinois provides compelling support for the importance of collegiality in building a professional culture of teaching on the one hand and in enhancing commitment and performance on the other. Both researchers found that the kind of leadership principals provided influenced the collegial norm structure of the school. Rosenholtz found that teachers in high-collegial schools describe their principals as being supportive and as considering problems to be schoolwide concerns that provided opportunities for collective problem solving and learning. Teachers and principals in less collegial schools, by contrast, reported being isolated and alienated.[1] In her research, Little found that norms of collegiality were developed when principals clearly communicated expectations for teacher cooperation; provided a model for collegiality by working firsthand with teachers in improving the school; rewarded expressions of collegiality among teachers by providing recognition, release time, money, and other support resources; and protected teachers who were willing to buck expected norms of privatism and isolation by engaging in collegial behaviors. [2]

> **When congeniality is combined with collegiality, work-enhancing values and norms are actually reinforced; but this ideal combination is not necessary for excellence.**

GETTING PRACTICAL FROM A MANAGEMENT PERSPECTIVE

Despite the evidence linking successful schooling with the development of a professional culture of teaching that supports and extends collegiality, many principals and superintendents remain hesitant. They recognize that the more collegiality is emphasized, the less appropriate will be many of the management practices that are now in place in our schools; but promoting collegiality is nothing more than being practical in a management sense. As work gets more complex, as the context of work gets less stable and more dynamic, and a structural looseness becomes more pronounced the only way in which work can be coordinated is through collaboration.

For example, fast-food restaurants, high-tech corporations, schools, and other organized enterprises have in common the need to coordinate different jobs, tasks, and responsibilities. Meeting this essential management requirement involves two contradictory strategies: assigning different responsibilities to different persons (what is known in management as differentiation) and bringing the work of these same people together to serve a common purpose (integration). Coordinating the work of people who have different responsibilities and/or who are located in different places is the way organizations achieve the needed integration. How management chooses to coordinate makes a difference. For an enterprise to function optimally, coordination strategies need to be matched with the degree of work complexity involved. If not, then the work will become simplified to match the coordination strategy, and performance will be negatively affected as a result.

> **Under direct and close supervision teachers teach according to the system's recipe; but when alone they teach in ways that make sense to them.**

McGill University management expert Henry Mintzberg points out that organizations have available four different coordinating strategies to ensure that responsibilities are met and work is brought together to serve a common purpose: directly and closely supervising workers; standardizing worker knowledge and skills; and relying on informal mutual adjustment that results from the need to cooperate (collaboration and collegiality).[3]

As the work of the organization changes from simple and straight-forward to complicated and dynamic, the coordinating strategy needs to change. Direct supervision and standardizing of both work processes and outcomes are appropriate and effective for organizations having simple work (the factory, the fast-food restaurant) but not for more complex organizations (medical teams, high-tech companies, schools). Enhancing and standardizing the knowledge base and relying on collaboration and collegiality is more appropriate for these more professional work settings. The reasons are practical ones. The loose connectedness of complex organizations does not make it possible to directly supervise what people are doing. Standardizing the work results in work simplification and in a less sophisticated, poorer quality product. For example, under direct and close supervision teachers teach according to the system's recipe; but when alone they teach in ways that make sense to them. When faced with an attempt to standardize their work, teachers resist by giving the appearances of complying.

When teachers are not able to resist close supervision and work standardization any longer, something has to give and invariably the work of teaching changes from situational and complex to simple and routine. This reality is a play on the old adage "form must follow function or function will follow form." Unfortunately, simplifying and routinizing the work of teachers will not provide the quality of schooling needed to serve this country well in tomorrow's increasingly complex world. Given this reality, building and enhancing norms of collegiality and providing the organizational arrangement that encourages collaboration become matters of managerial practicality.

OPPORTUNITY AND CAPACITY ARE KEY

Writing in the award-winning *Men and Women of the Corporation*, Rosabeth Moss Kanter pointed out that direct supervision, standardization practices, and other bureaucratic means of seeking coordination do not control what one does as much as they control what one cannot do. Such practices restrict the range of options available to teachers and principals. Fewer options means that teachers and principals will be less likely to respond to the intellectual challenges and academic demands they face on the one hand and to the unique needs and requirements of students and parents on the other. Everyone loses as a result. Limiting options of teachers and principals is bad educational policy.

As a result of her research Kanter found that "opportunity" and "power" were the essential characteristics necessary for effective performance in complex work. Opportunity refers to the perception teachers and principals have of the future prospects for advancement, increased responsibility, status, prestige and challenging work on the one hand and for increasing knowledge, skills and rewards on the other. Power refers to "the ability to get things done, to mobilize resources, to get and use whatever it is that a person needs for the goals he or she is attempting to meet." Kanter notes that too little opportunity[4] and power results in the rapid decay of whatever interest and excitement exists in one's job.

Stanford University researchers Milbrey Wallin McLaughlin and Sylvia Mei-Ling Yee point out that a collegial school environment enhances both levels of opportunity and capacity (their label for Kanter's power) for teachers, resulting in greater stimulation at work and higher levels of work motivation. They found that a teachers's effectiveness in a classroom, job satisfaction, and professional growth were directly linked to the opportunities they had to develop basic competence; the availability of weekend workshops or afterschool staff development sessions. Many factors—both informal and formal—comprise important opportunities. Our teachers mentioned . . . attending conferences, participating in informal mentor relationships, sharing ideas with other teachers; observing other classes and being observed . . ."[5] Teachers in their study commented as follows:

> "I'd like more people to come and visit my classroom—to look, visit, comment. Not to visit with an evaluative purpose, but with the purpose of commenting on what's going on in the classroom. I'd really like feedback from my peers."
>
> "I want nonthreatening feedback from someone who has the time to really take a hard look. It would have to be someone whom I respected and looked up to, and they would have to value the same things I do in teaching. I need a comfort zone, a framework around me within which I have the freedom to be myself—to use my own judgment and get trust and respect."
>
> "Coming to this school (with its high level of collegial interaction) had a tremendous impact on my attitude as a teacher. I found the staff as a whole more happy, more excited about teaching, more creative. In turn I became more excited and innovative about my own teaching . . . and less drained at the end of the day."[6]

Opportunity and capacity were the ingredients Seattle's Montlake Elementary School principal Lavaun Dennett provided in building a collegial faculty. Though satisfied with the faculty and believing that Montlake was a good school, she felt that the school was not working to full potential. She spent an entire summer working with the district Director of Special Education and the assistant superintendent coming up with a plan to radically restructure the school in a way that would dramatically reduce class size. This would be accomplished by using all of the teachers in the building to teach a "regular" classroom of students without pullout classes for Special Education (Chapter 1). As Dennett notes, prior to the start of the school year:

We organized a two day staff workshop and sent the staff an invitation. "How would you like to have class sizes of 20 students? How would you like to see every child in your class successful? "They came.Eager, Laughing, incredulous.

After two days of talking about the model and planning next steps, The staff could hardly wait for school to get started. Shortly afterwards, the Seattle Education Association went on a 19-day strike! We talkedout the window and on the sidewalk and continued the planning and preparation. We sent wonderful letters to parents telling them what a great year we had planned. We waited. And we waited. Finally the Education Association got an acceptable settlement and we went to work. Never had the work been so exciting. Or so rewarding. In many ways the staff worked harder than ever before. They spent extra hours after school in training and planning sessions, usually without pay.They spent more time communicating with one another and with parents. They created new lessons. They went to workshops and brought back new ideas.

Dennett reports that the change in students was even more dramatic. "Test scores went up dramatically, smiles became more and more contagious. Kids were so successful in classes that they stopped getting referred to Special Education."

In spite of its importance in enhancing both opportunity and capacity for teachers, collegiality does not come easy to Americans. Our culture tends to pride independence, self-reliance and competition over cooperation and interdependence, self-reliance and competition over cooperation and interdependence. This tradition does not encourage the building of norms of collegiality around group loyalty and other values of congeniality. Collaboration U.S. style needs to be built around ideas, values, beliefs, and commitments. Americans work together when we share common commitments and purposes and when we believe in the same goals. This commonness of purpose and commitment emerges in part from an established professional culture and in part from purposing provided by value-added leadership.

Purposing can be viewed as a compass that points the direction for a school or as a road map that details the way. In loosely connected schools engaged in complex work the compass view fits better. Harvard Business School Professor, Robert H. Hayes explains: "when you are lost on a highway, a road map is very useful; but when you are lost in a swamp whose topography is constantly changing, a road map is of little help. A simple compass—which indicates the general direction to be taken and allows you to use your own ingenuity in overcoming various difficulties—is much more valuablee."[7] When organizations are driven by the "compass" of purpose, collegiality becomes the strategy for achieving the needed coordination. Teachers and principals bonded together in a shared commitment decide what to do in the face of changing events by interacting with each other as colleagues as they work.

TEAM LEADERSHIP CAN HELP

When he was principal of the Webster school in New Rochelle, New York, Robert J. Stephens was able to enhance both purposing and collegiality by demonstrating a commitment to shared leadership. Ignoring union regulations and personnel office practices he decided to involve teachers in the recruitment and hiring of staff at Webster. He began by asking for volunteers from among the faculty who would serve on a school-based selection committee. Nor surprisingly this invitation was met with suspicion. The teachers just didn't believe that Stephens meant what he said in asking for their full participation. He did manage to get three teachers to reluctantly agree to serve.

> Getting extraordinary performance from teachers and principals requires throwing away policies and practices that are based on traditional conceptions of motivation.

Suspicion changed to enthusiasm as the process continued. The committee discussed and interviewed candidates, assessing both their competence and their fit with what the school represented. To do the job properly the teachers had to come to grips with what the Webster school stood for and what was meant by proper fit. This resulted in an emerging identity for the school that had a tremendous impact over the next several years. Soon teachers became competent at questioning. They looked for skills and competence. They learn to dismiss certain questions and began to ask more substantive, thought provoking questions which involved situations." Not only were classroom teachers involved in this process but members of the support staff and teacher assistants also participated thus providing a broader base of input into decisions in the building.

Webster became known as a team-based school and "people in the community began to view Webster teachers as a certain breed." Shared leadership, in this case, not only helped Webster come to grips with its basic purposes and commitment but provided a basis for building a sense of collegiality among the staff. As Principal Stephens would put it, "Our teachers think of each other as colleagues not competitors."

Corporate America has discovered anew the importance of the "people factor" in increasing competitiveness. What is different this time is the emphasis on recognizing people as key links to success— indeed as valuable resources for the corporation rather than just treating them "nice" to avoid problems. If you asked General Motors executive vice president Alan Smith what the winning ingredient was for corporate success he would respond:

> Technology? Very important.
> Capital? You've got to have it, and there's a lot around.
> Good plants and equipment? They're also important.
> But it's *people* that will make the difference.[8]

Smith believes that the company must set the climate for people to succeed by demonstrating by deeds as well as words that people are "our most important asset." To him this asset is best invested in excellence through teamwork. Principal Stephens would do very well as a manager at General Motors. By the same token lawmakers, state department of education, and local school district officials would take a giant step on the road to excellence if their policies followed the lead of Smith and Stephens. Opportunity and capacity, teamwork and collegiality when combined with purposing, leadership by outrage, and other dimensions of value-added leadership are the powerful ideas needed for building a professional culture of teaching aligned with excellence. One such additional dimension of value-added leadership is intrinsic motivation, the topic of the next section.

The Motivation Challenge

Intrinsic motivation plays an important role in value-added leadership. Too often, however, intrinsic motivation is confused with extrinsic, making the practice of this leadership difficult. American managers, for example, have been successful in getting required performance from workers; but the motivation challenge is to get extraordinary performance and on a sustained basis. Getting extraordinary performance from teachers and principals requires throwing away policies and practices that are based on traditional conceptions of motivation. Value-added leaders know that extraordinary commitment and performance over time cannot be brought, cajoled through clever leadership styles, forced by the rules, or achieved by controlling and inspecting. These traditional strategies can get people to do what they are supposed to but not more.

Extrinsic motivation is based upon the value a person receives from the external context of the work. Better working conditions, more money, a new title, prizes and awards, and compliments from supervisors are examples of extrinsic motivators. When extrinsically motivated teachers and principals are pushed by external rewards and punishments. "What gets rewarded gets done" is the philosophy. But their connection with the work they do is calculated. Work gets done as long as rewards are provided. When management cannot come up with the rewards desired by workers, they lessen their initiative and downgrade their performance.

Intrinsic motivation, by contrast, is based upon the value received from the work itself. Feelings of competence and achievement, excitement and challenge, meaning and significance, enjoyment and moral contentment that one receives from successfully engaging in the work are examples of intrinsic motivators. When intrinsically motivated, teachers and principals are pulled by an inner desire to be effective. "What is rewarding gets done, gets done well, and gets done on a sustained basis." Involvement with work is internal or moral or both.

Yale University professor, Robert J. Sternberg points out that "people who constantly need prodding or rewards or the fear of punishment to get tasks done are extrinsically motivated."[9] They work not because they believe in or enjoy the work but because they have to please others. "The biggest problem with extrinsic motivation is that it disappears when the rewards and punishments do."[10] When teachers are motivated by extrinsic means their involvement with work is calculated. A fair day's work is given for a fair day's pay and this rule is hardly a recipe for excellence in our schools.

THE HAZARDS OF RELYING ON EXTRINSIC REWARDS

What happens when extrinsic rewards are introduced in jobs where teachers and principals are already involved in intrinsically interesting and satisfying work? Is the work enhanced, diminished, or left unaffected by the introduction of these rewards? This is an important policy question because many efforts to improve schools rely on the introduction of extrinsic rewards. Edward L. Deci and Richard M. Ryan, two leading work motivation experts, conclude that the introduction of extrinsic rewards can actually diminish one's intrinsic interest in the work, resulting in reduced commitment and lower performance.[11] A person's involvement with work, for example, changes from internal and/or moral to instrumental and calculated. Work performance becomes dependent upon exchanges and bargains. Whether extrinsic rewards will backfire or not depends on whether teachers and principals view them as controlling or informational.[12]

> **Extrinsic factors such as money . . . can get people to do what they are supposed to but not more, at least not on a sustained basis.**

Rewards are viewed as controlling if they are intended to get workers to do something that the leader wants. They are viewed as informational if they are viewed as signals and symbols that a person is doing a good job and is appreciated. Throwing a party for a person, handing out buttons for good work, dishing out generous rounds of applause at faculty meetings, sending thank-you notes and so forth all have their place if they are given freely to communicate to teachers and others that they and their contributions are appreciated. The same rewards used to "motivate" a person to do something that the leader wants backfire. For this reason, extrinsic rewards need to be given with no strings attached. Furthermore, nominal extrinsic rewards are likely to work better than substantial ones. Giving a teacher a cash bonus as a sign of "appreciation," for example, is not likely to be viewed as informational but controlling, regardless of intent. The typical teacher asks "What do I have to do to get it? Now that I have it, what do they want in return?" Too often as a result, intrinsic and moral reasons for work give way to instrumental and calculated ones, with negative results for students in the long run. Extrinsic factors such as money do play an important role in obtaining and maintaining "a fair day's work for a fair day's pay." They are not, however, very good motivators of extraordinary commitment and performance. They can get people to do what they are supposed to but not more, at least not on a sustained basis.

The Secret of Motivation Is in the Work Itself

A number of well-known work researchers and management experts have pointed out that the secret to motivating extraordinary commitment and performance over time can only be found in the work itself. Though this understanding is well documented and widely accepted in work-motivation literature and is known to value-added leaders, it is too often ignored in school policies and practices.

Frederick Herzberg, for example, pointed out that such job factors as opportunity for and feelings of achievement and responsibility, interesting and challenging work, and opportunity for advancement have the capacity to motivate.[13] These factors are not something that leaders can give in turn for desired behavior but are an integral part of the work that one does. From their research Richard Hackman and Greg Oldman concluded that enhanced commitment and extraordinary performance were more likely to be present in the following situations:

• When workers found their work to be meaningful, purposeful, sensible, and significant; and when they viewed the work itself as being worthwhile and important.

• When workers had reasonable control over their work activities and were able to exert reasonable influence over work events and circumstances.

• When workers experienced personal responsibility for the work they did and were personally accountable for outcomes.[14]

To Mihaly Csikszentmihalyi enjoyment and "flow experience" are the keys to understanding intrinsic motivation. He studied highly accomplished and motivated experts in a number of different fields (i.e., rock climbers, surgeons, and composers). Though the work of these experts differed considerably each experienced a certain flow that Csikszentmihalyi attributes to intrinsic motivation. Flow is characterized by opportunity for action, the merging of action and awareness, focused attention characterized by concentration, narrowing of consciousness as one works, clarity of goals and norms, direct and immediate feedback, feeling of competence, and being in control of what one does.[15]

Though work psychologists have studied intrinsic motivation in different ways there is a convergence of opinion that the following are characteristics of jobs that enhance intrinsic motivation:

Allow for discovery, exploration, variety and challenge.

Provide high involvement with the task and high identity with the task enabling work to be considered important and significant.

Allow for active participation.

Emphasize agreement with respect to broad purposes and values that bond people together at work.

Permit outcomes within broad purposes to be determined by the worker.

Encourage autonomy and self-determination.

Allow persons to feel like "origins" of their own behavior rather than "pawns" manipulated from the outside.

Encourage feeling of competence and control and enhance feelings of efficacy.[16]

These characteristics must become the criteria for evaluating state mandates, school policies, and management practices if we want to achieve excellence.

INTRINSIC MOTIVATION AND STUDENT ACHIEVEMENT

Efficacy, intrinsic motivation, and commitment are qualities in teachers that are linked to gains in student achievement. In their study of the relationship between teachers' sense of efficacy and student achievement, for example, University of Florida researchers Patricia T. Ashton and Rodman B. Webb found the following when efficacy was high:

Teaching behaviors were characterized by warmth, accepting responses of students, accepting of student initiatives, and attention to students' individual needs.

Student behaviors were characterized by higher levels of enthusiasm and more initiation of interaction with the teacher.

Student achievement was higher in both high school mathematics and language basic skill test scores.[17]

A number of the value-added leadership dimensions discussed in this book that contribute to teachers' sense of efficacy, motivation and commitment are summarized in [Figure 1] that follows:

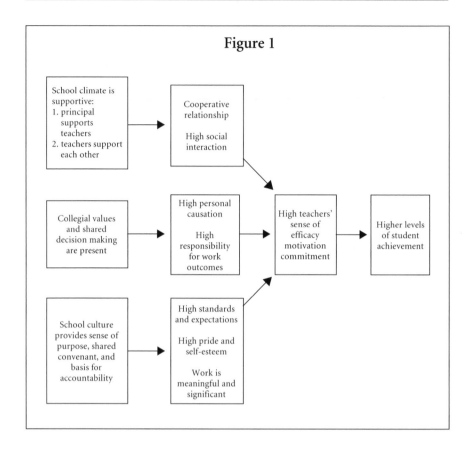

Figure 1

In few other areas are school leaders and policymakers on firmer grounds when relying on research than in the areas of teacher motivation and collegiality. Furthermore, this research is supported by the compelling realities of practice. Too often, however, policy mandates, administrative directives, and our own comfortable insistence on "business as usual" regarding school management and structure results in conditions and practices that are at odds with what we know is right and effective. As a result, policies and practices encourage bureaucratic teaching, promote isolation, encourage privatism, and discourage cooperation. Decreases in teacher and principal motivation and commitment follow. Bridging the gap between present practice and what we know must be done is the challenge of leadership. If we are to respond to this challenge, collegiality and intrinsic motivation must play key roles in efforts by federal, state, and local authorities to improve our schools.

NOTES

1. Susan J. Rosenholtz, *Teacher's Workplace: A Social-organizational Analysis* (New York: Longman, 1989).

2. Judith Warren Little, *School Success and Staff Development in Urban Desegregated Schools: A Summary of Recently Completed Research* (Boulder, Colorado: Center for Action Research, 1981).

3. Henry Mintzberg, *The Structuring of Organizations* (Englewood Cliffs, NJ: Prentice Hall, Inc., 1979).

4. Rosabeth Moss Kanter, *Men and Women of the Corporation* (New York: Basic Books, 1977).

5. Mibrey Wallin McLaughlin and Sylvia Mei-Ling Yee, "School as a Place to Have a Career," *Building a Professional Culture in Schools,* Ann Lieberman. ed., (New York Teachers College Press, 1988).

6. Ibid., p. 35.

7. Robert H. Hayes, "Strategic Planning—Forward in Reverse?" *Harvard Business Review,* (Nov.-Dec. 1985), p. 114.

8. Alan Smith, Presentation to the University Club of Chicago, Illinois (December 6, 1988).

9. Robert J. Sternberg, *The Triarchic Mind: A New Theory of Human Intelligence* (New York: Viking Press, 1988). p. 297.

10. Ibid, p.279.

11. Edward L Deci and Richard M. Ryan, *Intrinsic Motivation and Self-Determination in Human Behavior* (New York: Plenum Press, 1985).

12. Ibid.

13. Frederick Herzberg, *Work and the Nature of Man* (New York: World Publishing Co., 1966).

14. J. R. Hackman and Greg Oldman, "Motivation Through the Design of Work," *Organizational Behavior and Human Performance,* vol. 16, no. 2, (1976).

15. Mihalyi Csikszentmihalyi, *Beyond Boredom and Anxiety* (San Francisco: Jossey-Bass, 1973).

16. In addition to Deci and Ryan: Herzberg; Csikszentmihalyi; and Hackman and Oldman cited above see Robert W. White, "Motivation Reconsidered: The Concept of Competence." *Psychological Review,* vol. 66, no. 3, (1959) and Richard De Charms Personal Causation, (New York: Academic Press, 1968).

17. Patricia T Ashton and Rodman B. Webb, *Making a Difference: Teachers' Sense of Efficacy and Student Achievement* (New York: Longman, 1986).

18. Thomas J. Sergiovanni and Robert J. Starratt, *Supervision: Human Perspectives* (New York: McGraw Hill, 1988), p.135.

Small Schools, Great Expectations

Thomas J. Sergiovanni

> What's wrong with our schools today? Maybe the answer, in brief, is that they are too big.

Last year, newspapers across the country carried a story about a Dayton, Ohio, school's response to crowding and crime:

> The lockers are being bolted shut, and backpacks are being banned next month at Wilson Junior High School. . . . Instead of having to haul around textbooks, students will be given a set to keep at home, and classrooms will contain another set . . .(The principal) hopes the plan will lessen congestion during class changes; cut tardiness; reduce hiding places for guns, drugs, and other contraband; eliminate locker thefts; decrease the number of lost books; and help forgetful students (Associated Press 1994).

The school board's decision "to plunk down an additional $25,000 in local tax money to pay for duplicate books" came at an unfortunate time, the article noted, in that the state was short $100 million to buy updated textbooks.

In San Antonio, one school district copes with discipline problems by requiring junior and senior high school students to carry only transparent backpacks and book bags so that the contents are visible. Other school districts in the area have taken a high-tech approach, installing video cameras in 60 buses. According to a local paper, "The videotapes will be reviewed regularly, and can be used as evidence in student disciplinary actions" (Martinez 1994, p. 5b).

From *Educational Leadership,* vol. 53, no. 3, November 1995, pp. 48–52. © 1995 by Educational Leadership. Reprinted with permission.

Imagine the reaction if these were the banner newspaper stories when we went to school. Yet in this age of school detectors, such articles hardly raise eyebrows. Harsher times call for more desperate measures. But does it have to be this way? Perhaps in addressing problems of discipline (and learning as well) we should pay more attention to another aspect of schools: the way we organize them and build them (Sergiovanni. In press).

LEARNING COMMUNITIES

Recently, the Carnegie Foundation for the Advancement of Teaching proposed a new model for the elementary school that "connects people to people to build community; connects elements of the curriculum to achieve coherence; and connects learning to life to build character." A good school, the report concludes, should be small enough for everyone to know one another by name (Boyer 1995).

Of course, no single solution will make all students eager learners and caring members of their school. But there is a growing consensus that whatever else is done, schools must also become places where it is easier for students and teachers to know one another well and for students to connect to the school and its purposes. Schools, in other words, must become caring and learning communities, and community building is easier in small schools.

Communities are, in essence, places where members are bonded to one another by mutual commitments and special relationships, where they share a set of ideas and values that they feel compelled to follow. People belong and feel responsible for themselves and for others.

As school superintendent Joanne Yarvin says,

> The framework of operation must be small, physically close to children, and flexible. . . .
> We need small schools or schools that are divided into small community units; classroom time, space, and organization that allows personal relationships to flourish (1994).

Yarvin believes that educators must become today's "catchers in the rye," to use a metaphor from J. D. Salinger's novel of that name, and that it is only in small-scale schools that educators can "catch children who stray too close to the edge."

> Where schools are failing, it is not because they don't have enough projects and programs, but because they have lost the human touch.

Children mired in the morass of family and community decay can't benefit from red ribbons, higher standards, or instructional technology; they need caring adults to pull them out of the muck and set them on solid ground one at a time (1994).

NOT A MATTER OF FORM

In defining schools as small collections of people who are committed to one another and who share similar values and ideas, we may have to abandon the traditional brick-and-mortar conception of a school. Small schools can take many forms. Some can be housed in their own building, designed or remodeled to handle fewer students. Or, several independent schools with different purposes could function side by side in the same building.

This latter arrangement raises important questions, of course. How will such schools be managed? How will they share resources? What do we do about the football team, the band, and other sports and activities? Who will be responsible for the cafeteria? To which school will the librarian be assigned? Who reports to whom? And how will we decide which students and teachers go where?

One model worth thinking about is the office building. Here, a detective agency may share the first floor with a dentist's office; while an insurance agency occupies the second floor, a real estate agency, the third; and two more dentists' offices, the fourth. The lower level may be vacant, but available for rent. These enterprises share the same parking lot, maintenance staff, elevator service, security, and cafeteria; and they must follow the same health and safety codes and civil rights laws. But they set their own calendar and hours; hire, evaluate, and develop their own employees; and have their own dress codes and ways of doing things.

I doubt a school district would have problems working things out if it rented that lower level for a small elementary school that serves downtown commuters. So why would it be different if that district rented or owned the whole building, and put a different school on each floor? As with the dentists and their patients, students and their parents, together with teachers, could decide for themselves where to go.

IS SMALLER BETTER?

In *A Place Called School,* John Goodlad (1984) concluded that the burden of proof is on large size. Data from a study he conducted demonstrated that the smallest schools were better at solving their problems, more caring teachers and greater parent and student satisfaction. "It is not impossible to have a good large school," Goodlad observed, "it is simply more difficult" (p. 309).

As a result of his study of New Jersey high schools, W. J. Fowler reached a similar conclusion. He noted that student outcomes are more favorable in smaller public schools, and also in smaller districts (Fowler 1989).

Twenty-five years earlier, Roger Barker and Paul Gump, in *Big School, Small School* (1964), contended that a school should be small enough that all its students feel needed and, in fact, we needed to make the school work. As a result, students' school lives have more sense and meaning. Barker and Gump also found that students in smaller schools were more eager to earn, and more likely to participate in school activities.

Another important advantage of small schools, according to Judith Kleinfield (1993), is that they create "undermanned settings" where there are not enough people to fit all the available leadership roles. Consequently, more is asked of everyone, and students' learning curves are steeper as new challenges must be accepted, and new ideas mastered.

HOW SMALL IS SMALL?

A high school serious about preparing students for college, said James Conant in *The American High School Today* (1959), needs no fewer than 100 students in its graduating class. This has become the rule of thumb that many use in arriving at an optimum figure of about 400 students for a high school.

Douglas Heath (1994) recommends a range of 200–350 students for a lower school and 400–500 students for a high school. He believes that when these ceiling are exceeded, students and teachers alike have fewer opportunities for sustained relationships, resulting in an impersonal and bureaucratic climate:

> Students see their friends less frequently, have less contact with adults other than their teachers, participate much less frequently in extracurricular activities, including athletic teams, have much less opportunity to hold leadership positions, are more aggressive and disorderly, and cheat more frequently. Parents no longer visit the school as frequently or know their children's teachers as well (p. 81).

John Goodlad (1984) spoke favorably of the 225–250 student size of the British Infant School. As he put it,

> Indeed, I would want to face the challenge of justifying a senior, let alone a junior, high school of more than 500 to 600 students (unless I were willing to place arguments for a strong football team ahead of arguments for a good school, which I am not) (p. 310).

SMALL CHANGE?

The conventional wisdom is that bigger schools offer economies of scale that not only increase learning but save the taxpayers money. But the evidence points in the opposite direction. It appears that large schools are actually more expensive to operate.

Recently, the New York City-based Public Education Association and the Architectural League of New York examined the feasibility of operating small schools in New York City. The schools would not be alternative schools, but mainstays of the system. The two groups issued several reports that disprove the economy-of-scale argument. In *Small Schools' Operating Costs* (1994), the Public Education Association reported that

> no research evidence supports the claim that large schools of the size found in New York City (for example, 1,500 to 4,000 or more) achieve operational cost-scale efficiencies significant enough to justify their existence or to offset size-related, educationally damaged inefficiencies. On the contrary, studies show *diseconomies* (penalties) of scale in large schools. Difficult to manage efficiently and safely, large schools require . . . extra layer of managers . . . supervisors, assistant principals, deans, additional secretaries . . .

The report concludes that building schools with as few as 400 seats is cost-competitive with large-school construction. In a joint report on *Schools for New York,* the association and Architectural League (1994) present drawings by 52 teams of architects and designers showing what cost-effective small schools might look like. The construction specialists note that even more money could be saved by remodeling existing buildings or adapting existing non-school buildings for school use.

Tom Gregory has pointed out that the lower student-to-nonteacher ratio in smaller schools affords a key cost saving. To lower this ratio, he recommends that schools be modeled after cottage industries rather than corporations and other formal organizations.

He offers this scenario:

> The average per-pupil expenditure in this country is now about
> $5,260 per year. Envision a small, highly autonomous school, given
> that funding level. If the school has 200 kids in it, its annual operating
> budget is about $1,050,000. Return 20 percent of that amount—
> $210,000—to a trimmed-down central administration for its reduced
> services, and for bus transportation.
>
> Imagine a low student-teacher ratio, say 20 to 1. Pay your 10
> teachers well, say an average of $45,000 a year. Hire a head teacher,
> and pay him or her $60,000. Find an appropriate building and rent it
> for $7,000 a month plus another $3,000 for utilities. Hire a secretary, a
> custodian, and a cleaning person at $20,000 each. Budget $1,000 for
> supplies for each teacher, and $3,000 for the central office.
>
> Put aside $10,000 to buy books each year, and $20,000 for com-
> puters and A-V equipment. If the idea of (field) trips is appealing,
> lease three vans, each at $7,000 a year. That's probably enough to
> cover their maintenance, but include another $3,000 just to be sure.
> Put aside $12,000 to subsidize the fuel costs of trips.
>
> Now comes the fun: figuring out what to do with the $70,000 that
> has yet to be spent (Gregory 1992, p. 17).

Of course small schools should be valued because they are better
for students and better teachers, not simply because they save money.
It just so happens, however, that as some say, more productive. And
productivity divided by cost is the classic determiner of efficiency. In
fact, even if a small school *did* cost a little more than a large school, it
would still be more efficient if it were more productive.

THE PAROCHIAL MODEL

Catholic schools and other independent schools, which tend to be
smaller than their public school counterparts, have much to teach us.
True, many such schools are choosy about who they let in, preferring
students from privileged families and circumstances. But there are
also Catholic schools in inner-city areas serving children of the
underclass, and I am impressed with how well these schools are doing
with these students.

One advantage of parochial schools is that parents choose to
send their children there, and nearly all Catholic schools are able to
let parents know what is expected of their children and

It is not impossible to have a good large school; it is simply more
difficult to make these expectations stick. Mary Rivera, who has experience as a principal in both public and Catholic schools, sees two

other crucial advantages. Because these schools "don't follow the theory that larger is more efficient when it comes to education, "they can more easily build community. Above all, says Rivera,

> Parochial schools are K–8 schools (sometimes with pre-school, too) that keep families in the same place for a very, very long time. The people in them feel personal ties. The parents know all the teachers and the administrators, and those professionals know the whole family.

Rivera notes that parochial schools weren't always unique in this respect:

> Public schools used to be community/neighborhood-based at all grades. They *were* the center of neighborhood life. Everyone knew everyone. Even now, notice the uproar ever time a district redistributes kids to schools, or implements some busing plan that's supposed to improve education for someone (1994).

CONCRETE EXPRESSION OF BUREAUCRACY

Behind this discussion is a haunting question: If small schools and small classroom settings are good for students and good for our pocketbooks, why do we continue to operate and build large schools? Perhaps it is because committing to smaller schools would require us to rethink the theories of leadership, management, and organization that now dominate school administration. In small schools, there would be no need for elaborate administrative structures and hierarchies. The roles of assistant principal and middle manager would have to be reevaluated. Counseling and social work would be more informal. In short, we would have to make some tough decisions about our present allocation of resources and personnel.

Superintendent Yarvin believes we need small schools that put "authority in the hands of frontline practitioners," enabling them to "make exceptions to rules and change foolish ones".

> I have lost faith in any and all largescale, organized solutions to educational problems. They just put more paperwork, regulations, and job titles between children and the help they need (1994, p. 37).

Small size is a tough choice, but it is also the right choice because it helps us to see the small picture better. Nancy Webster, who has taught in Miami for 25 years, believes it is the small picture that counts big for students:

This really Big picture is full of problems I know but can't fix and vocabulary I understand but can't use; competency-based curriculum, authentic assessment, CORE, Total Quality Management, whole language, and a lot of other words. . . .

I've seen the vocabulary change, the classes get larger, the programs come and go, and more children fail. Meanwhile, 'at-risk' children have entered our vocabulary, along with 'dysfunctional families.'

Schools with over 1,000 elementary students are big business.

It's too bad, really, because schooling is . . . small, simple, and focused, when done well (1994, p. 52).

Perhaps we can use this small, simple, and focused school as a key leverage point for alleviating the alienation of students and making them more eager learners. If we succeed, surveillance cameras and transparent backpacks will no longer be necessary.

REFERENCES

Architectural League of New York and the Public Education Association. (1994). *Schools for New York: Plans and Precedents for Small Schools,* New York.

Associated Press. (July 11, 1994). "Dayton School Bans Lockers, Backpacks." *San Antonio Express News.*

Barker, R. G., and P. V. Gump. (1964). *Big School, Small School: High School Size and Student Behavior.* Stanford, Calif.: Stanford University Press.

Boyer, E. (1995). *The Basic School: A Community For Learning.* Princeton, N.J.: Carnegie Foundation for the Advancement of Teaching.

Conant, J. (1959). *The American High School Today: A First Report to Interested Students.* New York: McGraw Hill.

Fowler, W. J., Jr. (1989). "School Size, School Characteristics, and School Outcomes." Paper presented at the annual meeting of the American Educational Research Association, San Francisco.

Goodlad, J. (1984). *A Place Called School: Prospects for the Future.* New York: McGraw Hill.

Gregory, T. (September 1992). "Small Is Too Big: Achieving A Critical Anti-Mass In the High School." A position paper prepared for the Herbert H. Humphrey Institute For Public Affairs and the North Central Regional Educational Laboratory.

Heath, D. (1994). *Schools of Hope: Developing Mind and Character in Today's Youth.* San Francisco: Jossey-Bass.

Kleinfeld, J. (April 14, 1993). "No Shortage of Characters In the North." *Fairbanks Daily News Miner.*

Martinez, R. (August 14, 1994). "New School Year Brings Change." *San Antonio Express News.*

Public Education Association. (1994). *Small Schools' Operating Costs—Reversing Assumptions About Economics of Scale.* New York: Public Education Association.

Rivera, M. (January 26, 1994). "Neighborhood Schools: One Short Route To Reform." *Education Week* 13, 18: 39–40.

Sergiovanni, T. J. (In press). *Leadership for the Schoolhouse: How Is It Different? Why Is It Important?* San Francisco: Jossey-Bass.

Webster, N. (August 3, 1994). "The Big Picture For Little People." *Education Week.*

Yarvin, J. (September 14, 1994). "Catchers in the Rye." *Education Week.*

Index

Training and Publishing Inc.

We Prepare Your Teachers Today
for the Classrooms of Tomorrow

Learn from Our Books and from Our Authors!

Ignite Learning in Your School or District.

SkyLight's team of classroom-experienced consultants can help you foster systemic change for increased student achievement.

Professional development is a process, not an event. SkyLight's seasoned practitioners drive the creation of our on-site professional development programs, graduate courses, research-based publications, interactive video courses, teacher-friendly training materials, and online resources—call SkyLight Training and Publishing Inc. today.

SkyLight specializes in three professional development areas.

Specialty #

Best Practices

We **model** the best practices that result in improved student performance and guided applications.

Specialty #

Making the Innovations Last

We help set up **support** systems that make innovations part of everyday practice in the long-term systemic improvement of your school or district.

Specialty #

How to Assess the Results

We prepare your school leaders to encourage and **assess** teacher growth, **measure** student achievement, and **evaluate** program success.

Contact the SkyLight team and begin a process toward long-term results.

Training and Publishing Inc.

2626 S. Clearbrook Dr., Arlington Heights, IL 60005
800-348-4474 • 847-290-6600 • FAX 847-290-6609

There are

one-story intellects,

two-story intellects, and three-story

intellects with skylights. All fact collectors, who

have no aim beyond their facts, are one-story men. Two-story men

compare, reason, generalize, using the labors of the fact collectors as

well as their own. Three-story men idealize, imagine,

predict—their best illumination comes from

above, through the skylight.

—*Oliver Wendell*

Holmes

Training and Publishing Inc.